SEASIDERS AT

From the Empire to the Arch

A record of every player to have played at the Empire or New Wembley Stadium while playing for Blackpool Football Club.

Author: John Spooner

Dedication

This book is dedicated to those who introduced me to the roller coaster ride that Blackpool Football Club always seem to be on. Firstly my dad, who took me and my younger brother to Bloomfield Road for the first time on 28 October 1967 to witness a 1 0 home defeat at the hands of Queens Park Rangers. Secondly, my Grandad who became my regular matchday companion in my early years and introduced me to the delights of the spion kop.

Foreword

*"An appearance at Wembley is like a Command Performance.
It is a sign that a player has arrived. He has achieved the goal
most professionals dream about, yet so few rarely achieve"*

Harry Johnston, The Rocky Road to Wembley,

first published 1954

Acknowledgements

I must acknowledge the help and support received over the time spent putting this project together. Aside from the resources listed in my bibliography I place on record my thanks and appreciation to those who have provided input and advice along the way. Namely my youngest daughter Ellie, Jim Pyper my mentor from my sports quiz days, Glen Isherwood, author of one of my primary resources and to my brother David for the memory invoking art work on the front cover.

Introduction

At the time my interest in football began, in the late 60s, Wembley Stadium was considered the Holy Grail of English football. Everyone wanted to go there, as a player or supporter, but very few had the opportunity. As a professional footballer in 1967, the opportunity would only arise if their team reached a cup final, or they were selected for their national team to play for or against England

With so few games played there, the aura of the venue was understandable. A visit to Wembley was special and could create memories that last a lifetime. Nowadays, with Wembley hosting non-league finals, FA Cup semi-finals and EFL play-off finals there are more opportunities for players to play there and for supporters to attend games there.

Even so, it remains a magical place as supporters make the walk-up Olympic Way to the stadium soaking up the atmosphere. Fans stop to take selfies with the stadium as the backdrop or bump into someone they know or have not seen for years, stopping to discuss the achievement of their club in getting to Wembley, the state of their nerves and whether the ultimate dream of victory will be realised.

Having had the good fortune to visit the "Venue of Legends" old and new, on several occasions, it is fair to say no two visits are the same and, irrespective of whether the day has brought elation or disappointment, every single one has been memorable.

About this book

The aim of this book was to record every appearance made by Blackpool players for club, country or otherwise at the old British Empire Stadium from its opening in 1923, to its closure in 1999 and, since opening in 2007, at the new Wembley Stadium.

Although the original stadium was officially known as the Empire Stadium, in my experience, fans rarely referred to it by that name. For ease of reference, in this book, the stadium will be referred to as Wembley.

Part one of this book references the sixty fixtures involving Blackpool players starting with the first international appearance by a seasider at the stadium in 1939 up to and including the 2021 league one play-off final. Reference is made to the two near misses when the club has fallen at the last hurdle in pursuit of a Wembley appearance.

Part two of this book will provide reference to each of the one hundred and nine Blackpool players who have made an appearance for club and / or country starting with Jimmy Armfield, who made a club record sixteen appearances counting down to those who played at the old or new stadium just once.

Part three acknowledges the thirty-one players who, but for the decision to redevelop the stadium, would have appeared on the Wembley stage but found an alternative venue, the Millennium Stadium in Cardiff, on which to display their talents.

Throughout the book you will find headings such as Tangerine Trivia intended to highlight items of interest.

CONTENTS

The Empire Stadium

The Road to Wembley

Part one – the games

Wembley at War

After the War

The Golden Decade

1966 World Cup

Wembley opens its doors (wider)

A new Millenium

To the Arch (Wembley rebuilt)

Part two – the players

Part three – the Millenium men

Bibliography

THE EMPIRE STADIUM

The modern-day Wembley Stadium is, as the old stadium was, located in the town of Wembley in the county of Middlesex. The original stadium, named the Empire Stadium, was built to serve as the centrepiece of the British Empire Exhibition held in Wembley Park from 23 April 1924 to 31 October 1925. It took a total of 300 days to construct at an estimated cost of £750,000. The stadium was completed on 23 April 1923 just three days before the first football match held there, which became known as the White Horse Final, was to take place at the stadium.

The officially recorded attendance of 126,047 was far exceeded on the day leading to spectators spilling onto the pitch and the name came about due to the involvement of Billy, a White Horse, in controlling the crowd. Since that remarkable first day, the stadium played host to some memorable and historic sporting occasions of great interest to Blackpool supporters.

Following closure in 2000 demolition of the Empire Stadium finally began in 2002 enabling the new stadium to be built on the same land. The new Wembley Stadium was opened on 9 March 2007 with its official opening coming on 19 May 2007, the day of the FA Cup final. Less than 2 weeks later, on 29 May, the tangerine army invaded the new stadium for the first time to witness history as the seasiders returned to the second tier of English football after a twenty nine year absence.

THE ROAD TO WEMBLEY

From the opening of the Empire Stadium in 1923 until the outbreak of the Second World War the FA Cup Final, hosted annually, and the bi-annual England versus Scotland British Championship fixtures were the only major games played regularly at the stadium. The FA Cup, generally regarded as the greatest domestic cup competition in the world, had been hosted at multiple venues before 1923. From the date of the first FA Cup final hosted on 26 April 1923 the ambition of every club captain was to climb the thirty-nine steps and lift the famous trophy.

Although Blackpool never came close to winning the FA Cup in the pre-war years there is a link with the mighty Seasiders. Joe Smith, who captained Bolton Wanderers to a 2 0 win over West Ham United, in the first Wembley Cup Final in 1923, became manager of the Blackpool team that was such a force in the land in the 1940s and 50s, reaching the FA Cup finals of 1948, 1951 and 1953 before finishing first division runners-up in the 1955-56 season.

Often referred to as the Home International Championship, the British Championship was an annual international competition first contested in the 1883-4 season and last contested 100 years later by England, Scotland, Wales, and Northern Ireland. Each country played the other three throughout the season. Countries would alternate fixtures season by season with the England versus Scotland fixture the only one played bi-annually at Wembley until the mid-1950s when Wales, in the 1956-57 season, and Northern Ireland, in the 1957-58 season, made their competition debuts at the stadium.

In the 100 years of the British Championship, eleven different Blackpool players made a total of twenty-three Wembley appearances in the competition. Ironically the first and last of those appearances, given that Wembley is England's home venue, were made by Scotsman.

WORLD CUP AND EUROPEAN CHAMPIONSHIP QUALIFIERS

On occasions, the British Championship has doubled as a qualifying competition for the FIFA World Cup and UEFA's European Championship. In the 1949-50 season results doubled as qualifying results for the 1950 World Cup in Brazil. Similarly, in the 1953-54 season, results doubled as qualifying results for the 1954 World Cup in Germany.

Over the 1966-67 and 1967-68 seasons the results of the two championships were aggregated together to double as qualifying results for the quarter-final stages of the 1968 European Championship.

As time moved on more opportunities to play at the stadium arose. Wales and Northern Ireland became, like Scotland, bi-annual fixtures in the British Championship. The increasing number of friendlies played by national teams determined more international fixtures would be hosted at the stadium.

In 1967 the football league cup final was played there for the first time. In the 1980s the football league play-offs and the football league trophy became showpiece occasions. Since the 1990s FA Cup semi-finals have become regular fixtures there.

Part one – the games

This part of this book will provide reference to the sixty fixtures involving at least one Blackpool player who has made a Wembley appearance whether it be a charity fixture or a World Cup final. Reference is made to the two near misses when the club has fallen at the last hurdle in pursuit of a Wembley appearance.

1. England v Scotland – 9 April 1938

FRANK O'DONNELL – SCOTLAND

BRITISH CHAMPIONSHIP

So, who was the first seasider to play at Wembley Stadium? By the time England faced Scotland in 1938 thirteen international appearances had been made by six different players. With none of those appearances being made at Wembley, the distinction belonged to a Scotsman, Frank O'Donnell. Having established his reputation as a fearsome centre forward in Scotland he was signed by Blackpool from Preston North End for a fee of £10,000 in November 1937. He was selected to win the fifth of his six international caps, and his first as a Seasider, for Scotland in April 1938. With results confirming England as British Champions for the 25th time before the fixture, Frank helped provide the assist for Tommy Walker's goal to earn Scotland a 1 0 win and a tie for second place with Wales. In doing so he became the first seasider to have the pleasure of winning at Wembley.

9 April 1938 - England v **Scotland**		
	Player	Club
1	David Cumming	Middlesbrough
2	Andrew Anderson	Hearts
3	Andrew Beattie	Preston North End
4	Bill Shankly	Preston North End
5	Thomas Smith	Preston North End
6	George Brown	Rangers
7	John Milne	Middlesbrough
8	Thomas Walker	Hearts
9	**Frank O'Donnell**	**Blackpool**
10	George Mutch	Preston North End
11	Robert Reid	Brentford
	England 0 Scotland 1	

Tangerine trivia

In the days before substitutes squad members not selected in the starting eleven were referred to as reserves. Among the 're-serves' in the Scottish squad for the fixture were Seasiders Alec Munro and Willie Buchan. Making his Wembley debut in this fixture was one of the game's greatest players and future tangerine legend Stanley Matthews.

WEMBLEY AT WAR - 1939 to 1946

THE EMPIRE CLOSES ITS DOORS

With just one Blackpool player having had the opportunity to tread the Wembley turf, the start of the second world war brought about the closure of the Stadium. It didn't take long to recognise the impact of closing England's finest sporting venue. It was considered to have a demoralising effect on the British public. Thankfully, the impact was recognised by the government and the decision was reversed.

During the first world war, unofficial international fixtures had been played and the practice was revived. Between 11 November 1939 and 5 May 1945 England played 29 unofficial wartime internationals of which 8 were played at Wembley. With the games considered unofficial caps were not awarded determining that some great players made international appearances that do not feature in their national records.

2. England v Wales - 18 April 1940 - Dai Astley – Wales

The first seasider to feature in a wartime fixture at the famous stadium was David (Dai) Astley. Signed from Derby County in January 1939, Dai was a prolific scorer at international level. Capped at either inside right or centre forward he had scored 11 goals in 12 appearances for Wales before joining Blackpool.

Unfortunately, the outbreak of war restricted his goal scoring with the Seasiders to just 6 goals in 18 appearances, and 1 goal in his only official international appearance for Wales. Dai had played the opening three fixtures of the 1939/40 season when war was declared, and the season ended with Blackpool top of the first division. He continued to play for Blackpool during the war years and played in four wartime internationals for Wales.

The third of those games was the first Wartime international played at Wembley and the first appearance by a Welsh Representative side at the stadium. The early signs where the venue would become a happy hunting ground for Seasiders as, like Fank O'Donnell before him, Dai helped his team to secure a 1 0 win.

3. England v Scotland – 10 April 1942 "Jock" Dodds – Scotland

The second seasider to feature in a wartime international was also the second Scotsman to play at the stadium whilst a Blackpool player. Ephraim "Jock" Dodds was a goal-scoring centre forward who did not gain the international recognition his talents deserved until wartime. Jocks first Wembley appearance as a seasider was the fourth wartime international played at the stadium and ended in a goalless draw.

4. England v Wales 25 September 1943

Alex Roxburgh – England & Stan Mortensen – Wales

The sixth wartime international to be held at Wembley was the first to feature two Seasiders and the first to see Pool players in opposition. In goal for England in this eventful fixture was Alex Roxburgh who played for Blackpool during the 1930s and continued to do so during the war years before moving on to Barrow. This was to be his only international appearance in a game noted for a rather bizarre statistic!

The second seasider to feature in this game was the legendary Stan Mortensen. In the days before substitutes, Stan had been named as a reserve for the England team and attended the game in RAF uniform. As England developed the move leading to their first goal in the twelfth minute a Welsh defender, Ivor Powell, suffered a broken collarbone and could not continue. With no reserves available to the Welsh, it was agreed Morty would replace the injured Powell. Having changed out of his uniform Stan reappeared as England celebrated their second goal to make his unofficial international debut, for Wales!

Despite Morty's best efforts England lead 4 1 at half-time and went on to win the game 8 3 while Alex Roxburgh had the satisfaction of being on the winning side in his only international appearance. With Roxburgh starting the game and Morty's guest appearance there is a clear distinction as to who the fourth and fifth seasiders to play at Wembley were.

Three Lions trivia

Having made his wartime international debut for Wales Morty subsequently gained selection for England in several wartime internationals, although none of those games were at Wembley.

5. England v Scotland – 19 February 1944
"Jock" Dodds – Scotland

The final wartime international Wembley appearance by a seasider was a second appearance for their leading wartime goal scorer Ephraim "Jock" Dodd's. With a goalscoring record in wartime internationals to match his feats at club level, Jock became the first seasider to score at the stadium when netting a first-half equaliser for the visitors. However, five second-half goals, punctuated by a second goal for Jock saw England home to an emphatic victory

6. Combined Services v Police & Civil Defence – 9 May 1945
Stan Mortensen – Combined Services

An element of Wartime football was the use of the Stadium for charity fixtures. One such fixture was an annual game between the Combined Forces and the Police. With both teams comprising players from professional clubs the 1945 fixture was to be the last as players would return to their clubs as league football returned after the war

Having made his Wembley debut as a substitute for Wales in 1943 Stan Mortensen's position as a rear gunner in the RAF put him in contention to be selected for the Combined Services. With the services having a 100% record in the fixture Morty played his part in maintaining the record, scoring his first two Wembley goals in a 3 1 win for the Combined Services.

AFTER THE WAR

As recovery from the effects of the war began Blackpool Football Club were building towards the most successful decade in the clubs' history. During the war years, Blackpool had become one of the most watched teams in the land. With many top players posted in the area due to their service duties, they were able to guest for the club in wartime fixtures. One of these players, Stanley Matthews, had taken a shine to the area to the point where he had purchased a guest house in the town.

As competitive football was re-introduced pre-war stalwarts and future cup finalists such as Harry Johnston and Eric Hayward were back in the fold, Stan Mortensen had emerged as a forward with an eye for goal and todays much used phrase, player recruitment, had been effective as future international such as Eddie Shimwell and Hughie Kelly had been signed.

In May 1947 Joe Smith, Blackpool's manager, persuaded Stoke City to part company with the "Wizard of Dribble" for a fee of £11,500 and a huge building block in the path to the golden years had been cemented to add to those that were already there, such as Harry Johnston and Stan Mortensen .

Another building block and one of many bargain transfers from north of the border George Farm signed for Blackpool from Hibernian on a free transfer in September 1948. He proceeded to state his case as one of clubs greatest signings going on to exceed 450 football league appearance for the club.

7. England v Scotland – 12 April 1947

HARRY JOHNSTON – ENGLAND

BRITISH CHAMPIONSHIP

As football returned after the war the performances of the Seasiders most successful captain, Harry Johnston, had been noted by the England selectors and rewarded with selection for his country against Holland in November 1946. With England needing a point to secure the British Championship Harry was selected at left half to make the second of his ten international appearances and the first of his six Wembley appearances.

A fifteenth-minute strike by Preston North End debutant Andy McLaren for Scotland was cancelled out by Raich Carter of Derby County to secure the point England needed to win the Championship.

	12 April 1947 - England v Scotland	
	Player	Club
1	Frank Swift	Manchester City
2	Laurie Scott	Arsenal
3	George Harrdwick	Middlesbrough
4	Billy Wright	Wolverhampton W
5	Neil Franklin	Stoke City
6	**Harry Johnston**	**Blackpool**
7	Stanley Matthews	Stoke City
8	Raich Carter	Derby County
9	Tommy Lawton	Chelsea
10	Wilf Mannion	Middlesbrough
11	Jimmy Mullen	Wolverhampton W
	England 1 Scotland 1	

Three Lions Trivia

Alongside Harry Johnston, in the England team that day was Frank Swift of Manchester City who was born in Blackpool and the Wizard of Dribble, Stanley Matthews, then of Stoke City

Tangerine Trivia

Selection for this fixture made Harry Johnston the sixth Blackpool player to tread the Wembley turf and the second to do so in a British Championship fixture.

8. FA CUP FINAL – 24 APRIL 1948

BLACKPOOL V MANCHESTER UNITED

The Road to Wembley 1947-48

Home draws and convincing wins in the third, fourth and fifth round against lower league opposition saw the Seasiders into the last eight of the FA Cup for the first time and the quarter-final draw took them to Craven Cottage to face Fulham. Goals from Stan Mortensen and Jimmy McIntosh saw the Pool into their first semi-final against Tottenham Hotspur. Played at Villa Park a goal from Stan Mortensen was cancelled out by Len Dequeen and extra time was needed to separate the two sides. Two further goals from Mortensen decided the encounter and the Seasiders advanced to their first FA cup final.

R	V	Opponent	Res	F	A	Div
The Road to Wembley 1948						
3	H	Leeds Utd	W	4	0	2
4	H	Chester	W	4	0	3N
5	H	Colchester Utd	W	5	0	NL
6	A	Fulham	W	2	0	2
SF	N	Tottenham H	W	3	1	2
F	N	Manchester Utd	L	2	4	1

With Blackpool reaching their first FA Cup final nine Seasiders were making their first Wembley appearance while with the club. Although Stanley Matthews had graced the stadium many times before it was his first appearance at the stadium since joining Blackpool. Following his wartime appearances for Wales and the Combined Services Stan Mortensen was making his third appearance at the stadium while skipper, Harry Johnston, was making his second.

The game itself is regarded as one of the best FA Cup finals ever and generated some historic moments along the way. The award of a penalty kick to the Seasiders in the twelfth minute saw Eddie Shimwell become the first full-back ever to score in a final. With United equalising via a Jack Rowley goal in the twenty-fifth minute Stan Mortensen scored thirteen minutes later to become the first player to score in every round of the FA Cup.

Leading 2 1 at half-time Blackpool were well placed to win the FA Cup in their first Wembley appearance. Unfortunately, second-half goals from Jack Rowley, Stan Pearson and John Anderson saw the Seasiders become the first team to be beaten in an FA Cup final after taking the lead twice.

	1948 FA Cup Final
1	Joe Robinson
2	Eddie Shimwell
3	Johnny Crosland
4	Harry Johnston
5	Eric Hayward
6	Hugh Kelly
7	Stanley Matthews
8	Alex Munro
9	Stan Mortenson
10	George Dick
11	Walter Rickett

Tangerine Trivia

The first FA Cup Final appearance by Blackpool Football Club saw the club record number of Wembley debutants rise from two, in the 1943 war time international between England and Wales, too nine. Of the two players returning to the twin towers Morty was making his third appearance under the twin towers and Harry Johnston his second. Although Stanley Matthews was taking his Wembley appearance total into double figures it was his Wembley debut as a Blackpool player.

9. England v Scotland – 9 April 1949

STANLEY MATTHEWS - ENGLAND
STANLEY MORTENSEN - ENGLAND

BRITISH CHAMPIONSHIP

By the time the championship game against Scotland came round the two Stanley's, Matthews, and Mortensen were gaining regular selection for England and had played together for their country seven times. Their eighth partnership for the three lions was their first at Wembley.

A good start to the game by England saw Morty denied twice by Scotland keeper Jimmy Conan before the visitors took charge. Goals from Jimmy Mason, Billy Steel and Lawrie Reilly saw them leading 3 0 by the hour mark. As England fought back Jackie Milburn diverted a shot from Morty into the Scottish net to reduce the deficit. Despite constant England pressure, the visitors saw the game out to inflict England's first post-war defeat on home soil and win the British Championship for the twenty-fifth time.

Tangerine Trivia

Morty's appearance in this fixture was the fourth time he had graced the Wembley turf. Remarkably those four appearances had been made while playing for four different teams, Wales, the Combined Services, Blackpool and England. The Wizard of Dribble was making his second Wembley appearance as a Blackpool player.

	9 April 1949 - **England** v Scotland	
	Player	Club
1	Frank Swift	Manchester City
2	John Aston	Manchester United
3	John Howe	Derby County
5	Billy Wright	Wolverhampton W
5	Neil Franklin	Stoke City
6	Henry Cockburn	Manchester United
7	**Stanley Matthews**	**Blackpool**
8	**Stan Mortenson**	**Blackpool**
9	Jackie Milburn	Newcastle United
10	Stan Pearson	Manchester United
11	Tom Finney	Preston North End
	England 2 Scotland 3	

THE GOLDEN DECADE

Research and reflection around the history of Blackpool Football Club make it clear that, whatever happened before or since, the 1950s was the golden decade. While the 1953 FA Cup final win was the greatest moment in the clubs' history, the fact that seven members of that team also represented their countries at Wembley stadium examples the quality of the cup winning team. Records show a total of forty nine football matches were played at the stadium during the 1950's. Twenty-five of those fixtures included players who wore the tangerine and white of Blackpool Football Club.

Having started the decade with a cup run that ended in the quarter-final and a seventh-place finish it was clear the Seasiders were emerging as a major force in the land. For much of the 1950/51 season, they were genuine contenders for the league and FA Cup double which, at the time, had only been achieved once before by Preston North End in the 1888/89 season.

10.　England v Scotland – 14 April 1951

HARRY JOHNSTON - ENGLAND
STANLEY MATTHEWS - ENGLAND
STANLEY MORTENSEN – ENGLAND

BRITISH CHAMPIONSHIP

And then there were three! Two weeks before their second FA Cup final, Blackpool had three players in an England team. At this point, Matthews and Mortensen were fixtures in the national side while Harry Johnston was recalled winning his third cap four years after his second. With Blackpool having reached the FA Cup final it meant the three Seasiders would be playing at Wembley twice in as many weeks.

Despite being down to ten men after ten minutes due to injury England took the lead in the eleventh minute when Mortensen played in Huddersfield Town debutant Harold Hassall for the opening goal of the game. Having not lost a British Championship fixture at Wembley since 1934, and with a man advantage, Scotland came back strongly with goals from Bobby Johnstone, Laurie Reilly and Billy Liddell to lead 3 1 after fifty-five minutes.

With a thrashing a possibility England, with all three Seasiders prominent, came back strongly and with ten minutes remaining the Preston Plumber, Tom Finney, reduced the deficit to set up a barnstorming finish. Try as they might England could not find an equaliser and Scotland held on to win the game and claim the title of British Champions for a record-equalling twenty-ninth time.

	14 April 1951 - **England** v Scotland	
1	Bert Williams	Woverhampton W
2	Alf Ramsey	Tottenham Hotspur
3	Bill Eckersley	Blackburn Rovers
4	**Harry Johnston**	**Blackpool**
5	Jack Froggatt	Portsmouth
6	Billy Wright	Woverhampton W
7	**Stanley Matthews**	**Blackpool**
8	Wilf Mannion	Middlesbrough
9	**Stan Mortenson**	**Blackpool**
10	Harold Hassall	Huddersfield Town
11	Tom Finney	Preston North End
	England 2 Scotland 3	

Tangerine Trivia

With Harry Johnston, Stan Matthews and Stan Mortensen on England duty a double chasing Blackpool team were left to face Middlesbrough at Bloomfield Road and won the game 2 1.

11. FA CUP FINAL – 28 April 1951

BLACKPOOL V NEWCASTLE UNITED

The Road to Wembley 1950-51

Having lost to Liverpool on boxing day 1950 the Seasiders went on a run of 12 league games unbeaten. During that period, they had also played 7 FA cup ties which `saw them progress to their second FA cup final and in contention for the league title along with the likes of Tottenham Hotspur and Manchester United.

Having needed a replay to progress in the third round and made hard work of beating lower league opposition in the fourth and fifth rounds the Pool were drawn at home to their 1948 quarter-final opponents Fulham at the same stage of the 1951 competition. A single goal was sufficient to win the tie and progress to face second division Birmingham City in the semi-final. A replay was needed to secure a second FA Cup final appearance. A draw with their cup final opponents, Newcastle United, was followed by five consecutive league wins and with six games remaining the Seasiders were well placed in their pursuit of a possible double.

On 7 April, the 19-game unbeaten run ended with a 2 1 defeat away to Huddersfield Town. An unfortunate side issue of the defeat was a season-ending injury to Allan Brown which denied him of Wembley appearances for both club and country.

The Road to Wembley 1951						
R	V	Opponent	Res	F	A	Div
3	A	Charlton Athletic	D	2	2	1
3R	H	Charlton Athletic	W	1	0	1
4	H	Stockport County	W	2	1	3N
5	H	Mansfield Town	W	2	0	3N
6	H	Fulham	W	1	0	1
SF	N	Birmingham City	D	0	0	2
SFR	N	Birmingham City	W	2	1	2
F	N	Newcastle United	L	0	2	1

In addition to the triumvirate of Johnston, Matthews and Mortensen , Eddie Shimwell, Eric Hayward and Hughie Kelly were all making their second appearances ensuring there was plenty of Wembley and Cup final experience in the group. Being aware of the threat posed by Newcastle's legendary number 9, Jackie Milburn, the Pools tactical plan was to maintain a high defensive line with the intent of catching him and his fellow forwards offside.

Unfortunately, the plan failed when, with Blackpool threatening, a right-wing cut-back from Matthews was intercepted and the ball moved via two first time passes to Milburn. From inside his half, he outstripped the Blackpool defence and buried the chance to give Newcastle a fiftieth-minute lead. Five minutes later a clever backheel from Newcastle's number 8, Ernie Taylor allowed Milburn to unleash a shot from just outside the penalty area to settle the encounter and take the FA Cup back to the North East.

	1951 FA Cup Final
1	George Farm
2	Eddie Shimwell
3	Tommy Garrett
4	Harry Johnston
5	Eric Hayward
6	Hugh Kelly
7	Stanley Matthews
8	Jackie Mudie
9	Stan Mortenson
10	Bill Slater
11	Bill Perry

FA Cup Final hangover

Unfortunately, the hangover from the FA Cup final defeat saw the Pool take just 1 point out of their final 2 league games, while Tottenham and Manchester United finished strongly to claim first and second place, respectively. The Seasiders third-place finish, with a club-record first division total of 50 points, was their best league performance to date. Without a doubt, the Seasiders had arrived as a force in the land.

12. England v Argentina – 9 May 1951

STAN MORTENSEN – ENGLAND

FESTIVAL OF BRITAIN CELEBRATION MATCH

The Festival of Britain ran from 3 May to the end of September 1951 to commemorate the centenary of the Great Exhibition of 1851. The intent was to promote a sense the nation was recovering from the effects of the second world war and highlight its contribution to the arts, science and sport.

As part of the celebrations, England would play their first-ever international against Argentina and begin an incident-packed rivalry that remains alive today. Injuries and changes from the side that faced Scotland meant Stan Mortensen was the only seasider to retain his place and would play at Wembley for the third time in less than three weeks. Selected at centre forward against Scotland he switched to inside right to accommodate Newcastle's FA Cup goalscoring hero Jackie Milburn.

Played in front of a record crowd for a Wednesday afternoon international the South Americans drew first blood with an eighteenth-minute goal from Mario Boye. With ten minutes remaining England's unbeaten home record against foreign opposition was under threat when Morty diverted Halsall's goalward header from close range to equalise. With England pressing for the winner Morty was involved again when he chested a cross into the path of Milburn to net the winner and draw first blood for the three lions against their South American opponents.

9 May 1951 - **England** v Argentina		
	Player	Club
1	Bert Williams	Wolverhampton W
2	Alf Ramsey	Tottenham Hotspur
3	Bill Eckerseley	Blackburn Rovers
4	Billy Wright	Wolverhampton W
5	James Taylor	Fulham
6	Henry Cockburn	Manchester United
7	Tom Finney	Preston North End
8	**Stan Mortenson**	**Blackpool**
9	Jackie Milburn	Newcastle United
10	Harold Hassall	Huddersfield Town
11	Victor Metcalfe	Huddersfield Town
England 2 Argentina 1		

13. England v Scotland – 18 April 1953

GEORGE FARM – SCOTLAND

BRITISH CHAMPIONSHIP

To example how rare the opportunity to play at Wembley arose, following Morty's appearance against Argentina in 1951 it was nearly two years before another seasider, George Farm, appeared at the stadium. In between the two fixtures, the Empire Stadium had hosted just three full internationals plus the 1952 FA Cup final.

Having been selected to win his third cap for Scotland, George was making his second Wembley appearance and became the first Blackpool goalkeeper to be selected for a full international at Wembley. With Scotland unbeaten in full internationals at Wembley since 1934 and needing a win to claim the title of British Championship there was more than pride at stake. While a win would secure the title for Scotland, defeat would present the title to England. Twice Ivor Broadis gave England the lead and twice Laurie Reilly equalised for Scotland. A draw meant the auld enemy would share the title and that George Farm had had a good day. Two weeks later he would be back at Wembley for an even better one.

	18 April 1953 - England v **Scotland**	
	Player	Club
1	**George Farm**	**Blackpool**
2	George Young	Rangers
3	Sam Cox	Rangers
4	Tommy Docherty	Preston North End
5	Frank Brennan	Newcastle United
6	Doug Cowie	Dundee
7	Thomas Wright	Sunderland
8	Robert Johnstone	Hiberniian
9	Lawrie Reilly	Hiberniian
10	Billy Steel	Dundee
11	BillyLiddell	Liverpool
	England 2 Scotland 2	

Tangerine Trivia

With George Farm on international duty and Willie Hall making a rare first team appearance Blackpool beat Liverpool 3-1 at Bloomfield Road making it a good day all around

14. FA CUP FINAL – 2 May 1953

BLACKPOOL V BOLTON WANDERERS

As the calendar year of 1952 ended and 1953 began there were two recurring questions from the arena of sport. Would the twenty-six-time champion flat racing jockey Gordon Richards finally win the Epsom Derby and would Stanley Matthews, playing at an age when many players would have retired, claim the FA Cup winners medal he craved.

The Road to Wembley 1952-53

Compared to the FA Cup runs of 1948 and 1951 the road to Wembley in 1953 was possibly the hardest to negotiate. Every round produced tight games decided by one goal and the lowest-ranked team the Pool faced were Southampton, who were relegated from division 2 at the end of the 1952-53 season.

After holding the Seasiders to a draw in the fifth round at Bloomfield Road the Saints dominated the first-half of the replay at the Dell and lead 1 0 at half-time. In his autobiography, skipper Harry Johnston informed that both he and manager Joe Smith had stern words with the team at the interval. A second-half comeback saw the Pool turn it round and progress to a sixth-round tie against an Arsenal team who were genuine contenders for a League and FA Cup double.

When the sixth-round day arrived, the performance was on a different level as the Seasiders secured a deserved 2 1 win. Sadly, the delight was tinged with disappointment as Allan Brown broke his leg in the process of scoring the winner and would not play again that season. For the second time, the Seasiders faced Tottenham Hotspur in an FA Cup semi-final. With the score 1 1 and a replay on the cards Jackie Mudie intercepted a back pass and netted the goal that took the Pool to Wembley for the third time in five seasons. Would it be third time lucky?

The Road to Wembley 1953						
R	V	Opponent	Res	F	A	Div
3	A	Sheffield Wednesday	W	2	1	1
4	H	Huddersfield Town	W	1	0	2
5	H	Southampton	D	1	1	2
5R	A	Southampton	W	2	1	2
6	A	Arsenal	W	2	1	1
SF	N	Tottenham Hotspur	W	2	1	1
F	N	Bolton Wanderers	W	4	3	1

With the coronation of Queen Elizabeth just a month away the nation was caught up in a feel-good factor and the desire to rent or purchase a television in time for the big day was on the rise meaning more people would be able to witness the cup final than ever before. Coaches taking supporters to the final were decked out in tangerine and white and the question on many peoples lips was would Stanley Matthews finally claim an FA Cup winners medal at the age of thirty-eight.

With seven survivors of the 1951 Cup Final, there was plenty of matchday experience in the team. An eighth team member of the team, Ernie Taylor, had starred for Newcastle that day and was looking to claim a second winners medal. With just two minutes on the clock George Farm, making his third Wembley appearance just two weeks after his second was picking the ball out of the net as Nat Lofthouse emulated Stan Mortensen's 1948 achievement of scoring in every round of the FA Cup.

In many years of reading about or watching the Seasiders, it is clear the concession of an early goal can generate a roll your sleeves up moment and has the effect of focusing the mind. Sure, enough Stan Mortensen equalised in the thirty-sixth minute, only for Willie Moir to restore the Trotters lead three minutes later. Trailing at half-time a goal from the injured Eric Bell, ten minutes into the second-half, had surely put the game beyond Matthews and the team in tangerine?

As the game moved into its final quarter, the heat of cup final day and the toll of playing with an injured player was beginning to tell on the Wanderers. The court jester, Ernie Taylor, was finding the wizard of dribble, Stanley Matthews, with a stream of passes as Blackpool supporters hoped the spell would be cast and the tide would turn tangerine.

A scramble in the six-yard box saw Morty net his second goal of the game and with twenty minutes remaining it was game on. If the written word is to be believed the nation outside of Bolton, be they at the game, watching on television, or listening to the radio, were willing Matthews and Blackpool to find the equaliser.

With the clock ticking down an innocuous foul on Jackie Mudie was penalised and a free kick is awarded on the edge of the D. A defensive wall was lined up and, on first look, there was no way through to goal. The deliberations continue and, on a second look, a gap between wall and post is spotted by Morty who drilled the ball into the Bolton net and became the first player to score a hat trick in an FA Cup final. The scores were level and extra time beckoned for two weary teams.

As the clock moved past the ninety-minute mark Matthews and Wembley debutant Ernie Taylor manoeuvred the ball down the right wing to allow the Wizard to take on the Bolton left-back, Tommy Banks, once again. With a customary drop of the shoulder, Matthews beat his man and cut the ball back to Morty who was not there, but Bill Perry was. A crisp left-foot strike followed to register arguably the most significant goal in the history of Blackpool Football Club. The goal that won the FA Cup!

Moments later Harry Johnston, making his fifth Wembley appearance led his team up the thirty-nine steps to collect the famous trophy from Her Majesty the Queen. In the days before European competition winning the FA Cup was seen as a landmark achievement and now eleven footballers wearing the famous tangerine shirts had added their names to the list of players who had done it.

	1953 FA Cup Final
1	George Farm
2	Eddie Shimwell
3	Tommy Garrett
4	Ewan Fenton
5	Harry Johnston
6	Cyril Robinson
7	Stanley Matthews
8	Ernie Taylor
9	Stan Mortenson
10	Jackie Mudie
11	Bill Perry

A year to remember

In a final of twists, turns and footballing trivia Blackpool Football Club had delivered their command performance, and the FA Cup was off to spend a year beside the Irish sea.

A month later, on the second of June, the Coronation of Queen Elizabeth II took place. Four days later the newly crowned Queen hoped to celebrate by winning the Epsom Derby with her horse Aureole. In the event Her Royal Highness had to settle for second place as Gordon Richards quest for the "Holy Grail" of flat racing was realised when he rode Pinza to secure his one and only Derby win in his twenty-eighth (and final) attempt.

Tangerine Trivia – Ernie Taylor

Having played for Newcastle against Blackpool in 1951, Ernie Taylor had the distinction of playing for and against the Seasiders in the FA Cup final. In 1958, in the wake of the Munich disaster, he moved to Manchester United and became the first player to play in Wembley FA Cup finals for three different clubs. United were beaten 2 0 by Bolton Wanderers which meant Ernie had been on the winning and losing side in FA Cup finals against the Trotters.

Tangerine Trivia - Stan Mortensen

With a goal in the 1948 FA Cup against Manchester United, Morty's hat trick in 1953 made him the first player to have scored 4 goals in Wembley FA Cup finals. His record stood, individually until 1989 when Ian Rush equalled his tally with two goals against Everton and jointly until 1992 when Rush scored his record fifth FA Cup final goal against Sunderland.

Tangerine Trivia - Cyril Robinson

Signed from Mansfield Town in 1949 Cyril made just twenty-two first-team appearances for the Seasiders. Injury to Hughie Kelly meant the fifteenth of those appearances was made in an FA Cup final.

Not so Tangerine Trivia – Malcolm Barrass

Among the eleven trotters on the Wembley stage the responsibility of marking hat trick hero Stan Mortenson fell to Blackpool born Malcolm Barrass whose father Matt made more than 150 appearance for the Pool in the 1920s.

Not so Tangerine Trivia – Nat Lofthouse

By scoring Wanderers opening goal in the second minute Nat Lofthouse emulated Stan Mortensons 1948 achievements of scoring in every round and finishing on the losing side in an FA Cup final. Like Morty, he had his day some years later when scoring the 2 goals that saw the trotters beat Manchester United to win the Cup in 1958.

15. England v Rest of the World
21 October 1953

STAN MATTHEWS
STAN MORTENSEN

FOOTBALL ASSOCIATIONS 90th ANNIVERSARY
CELEBRATION INTERNATIONAL

To mark the ninetieth anniversary of the founding of the Football Association a fixture between England and team representing the Rest of the World was arranged to mark the occasion. With players drawn from five European countries, the naming of opposition was questionable. What was not in doubt was the abundance of talent in the players on view. With FA Cup winners Matthews and Mortensen on the England side the seaside interest was clear.

The concession of a first-minute penalty saw Ladislav Kubala give the Rest of the World side the lead. Never far from the action, the irrepressible Stan Mortensen levelled the scores in the seventh minute and a thrilling, goal-laden game was to follow. Two goals from the Italian Giampero Boniperti saw the Rest of the World take a 3 1 lead. As the half was ending England pulled a goal back and across from Matthews hit the bar following a misjudgement by the keeper.

Trailing 3 2 at half-time England started the second-half with Mathews setting up an equaliser and Mortensen going close on a couple of occasions. In what was an entertaining end to end game the Rest of the World took the lead for the third time when Kubala netted his second goal in the sixty-third minute. With a minute left and England's unbeaten home record against opposition from outside the British Isles on the line, a typical surge from Mortensen induced a clumsy challenge and the award of a penalty kick followed. To the delight of the home support, Alf Ramsey converted the penalty kick, and the unbeaten record was preserved with a 4 4 draw.

	Player	Club
	21 October 1953 - England v Rest of the World	
1	Gil Merrick	Birmingham City
2	Alf Ramsey	Tottenham Hotspur
3	Bill Eckersley	Blackburn Rovers
4	Billy Wright	Wolverhampton W
5	Derek Ufton	Charlton Athletic
6	Jimmy Dickinson	Portsmouth
7	**Stanley Matthews**	**Blackpool**
8	**Stan Mortenson**	**Blackpool**
9	Nat Lofthouse	Bolton Wanderers
10	Albert Quixall	Sheffield Wednesday
11	James Mullen	Wolverhampton W
	England 4 Rest of the World 4	

Three Lions trivia

Forty-six years after the completion of the fixture FIFA opted to downgrade it from the status of a full international as the game was not played against a national team. That could have resulted in the withdrawal of the England caps awarded for that fixture. Although the Rest of the World was a makeshift side, given the quality of the players involved it would rank above many national teams of the day.

On the date of the game the twelve players who represented the Rest of the World had amassed more than 350 international appearances for 8 different countries between them. Sensibly, the FA chose not to withdraw any awarded caps and continued to recognise the fixture as a full international

16. England v Hungary - 25 November 1953

HARRY JOHNSTON
STAN MATTHEWS
STAN MORTENSEN
ERNIE TAYLOR

FRIENDLY INTERNATIONAL

That Harry Johnston and Stanley Matthews both have chapters in their respective autobiographies dedicated to this specific fixture speaks volumes for the impact it had on them as players and on the game itself. Nearly seven months on from the greatest day in the history of Blackpool Football Club this game presented another landmark achievement for the club.

For the first time, four Seasiders were selected to represent their country. Harry Johnston, the cup winning captain was making his sixth Wembley appearance while the Wizard of Dribble, Stanley Matthews was making his eighth appearance while a Blackpool player. Ernie Taylor, the Court Jester as he was often known, was making his England debut and his second Wembley appearance as a seasider. Finally, hat trick hero Stan Mortensen was making his tenth appearance at the Empire Stadium.

In the days before the European Champions Cup not much was known about overseas players and clubs, particularly those from eastern Europe. At the time of their Wembley visit, the Magyars were unbeaten in twenty-four games. Having won Olympic Gold in 1952 their national selectors recognised the value of teamwork and were not afraid for one club to dominate team selection.

With seven players from Honved Budapest selected the team ethos was likely to be strong and within a minute one of the seven, Nandor Hidgeguti had given the visitors the lead. In the fifteenth minute, Morty presented Jackie Sewell with the opportunity to equalise. In seven minutes from the twentieth to the twenty-seventh minute, a second goal from Hidgeguti and two from Ferenc Puskas saw the visitors storm into a 4 1 lead. Despite being outclassed England continued to battle and on thirty-eight minutes Stan Mortensen netted his twenty-third goal for his country to reduce the arrears.

After a breathless first-half had ended with Hungary leading 4 2 there was little respite for the three lions. Within ten minutes of the second half a third Honved player, Jozsef Bozsik had found the net and Hidgeguti had completed a superb hat trick. Trailing 6 2 England's proud record of having never lost a home fixture to a side from outside the British Isles was in tatters.

The lions continued to battle resolutely, and Mortensen was brought down to earn England a penalty kick in the fifty-ninth minute. The kick was taken, and scored, by Alf Ramsey the man who would subsequently oversee the greatest moment in the history of English football.

At the end of the ninety minutes, Hungary had won 6 3 and the realisation that English football had to change was starting to sink in. in their autobiographies of Johnston and Matthews both admit to the superiority of the Hungarians on the day and acknowledge the complacency and deficiencies creeping into the English game. Sadly, three of the Seasiders fantastic four Johnston, Taylor and Mortensen had played their last game for England and made their final Wembley appearance.

	25 November 1953 - **England** v Hungary	
	Player	Club
1	Gil Merrick	Birmingham City
2	Alf Ramsey	Tottenham Hotspur
3	Bill Eckersley	Blackburn Rovers
4	Billy Wright	Wolverhampton W
5	**Harry Johnston**	**Blackpool**
6	Jimmy Dickinson	Portsmouth
7	**Stanley Matthews**	**Blackpool**
8	**Ernie Taylor**	**Blackpool**
9	**Stan Mortenson**	**Blackpool**
10	John Sewell	Sheffield Wednesday
11	George Robb	Tottenham Hotspur
	England 3 Hungary 6	

Tangerine Trivia

Having made his final international appearance Stan Mortensen had won his twenty fifth England cap. His three lions career ended with the distinction of being Blackpool's most capped international footballer until May 1955 when Stan Matthews won his twenty fifth and twenty sixth caps to equal and then pass Morty's record

Six months later

Naturally, some theorised that poor team selection and a difficult day at the office were the major factors rather than the superiority of the opposition. When the two sides met in Budapest six months later England suffered their heaviest international defeat, losing 7 1. For those who did not believe that change was necessary, they did now!

17. England v Wales - 10 November 1954

STANLEY MATTHEWS

BRITISH CHAMPIONSHIP

Although England had hosted Wales at Wembley during wartime, a full international between them was not held there until 1952. The first Blackpool player to feature in a full international match between the nations at the famous stadium was Stanley Matthews.

On a rain-sodden day, the Wizard of Dribble was heavily involved in the creation of goalscoring opportunities for Chelsea's Roy Bentley as his headers in the seventieth and seventy-sixth minutes turned a 1 0 deficit into a 2 1 lead. With ten minutes remaining the Welsh talisman, John Charles levelled the scores to set up an exciting climax.

Two minutes later, Bentley completed his hat trick from close range following Ronnie Allen's back heel and England went on to secure the win in an enthralling game of football.

	10 November 1954 - **England** v Wales	
	Player	Club
1	Ray Wood	Manchester United
2	Ron staniforth	Huddersfield Town
3	Roger Byrne	Manchester United
4	Len Phillips	Portsmouth
5	Billy Wright	Wolverhampton W
6	Bill Slater	Wolverhampton W
7	**Sranley Matthews**	**Blackpool**
8	Roy Bentley	Chelsea
9	Ronnie Allen	West Bromwich Albion
10	Len Shackleton	Sunderland
11	Frank Blunstone	Chelsea
	England 3 Wales 2	

Tangerine trivia

Bill Slater, who played for Blackpool in the 1951 FA Cup final against Newcastle United made his England debut in this match.

18. England v Germany - 1 December 1954

STANLEY MATTHEWS

FRIENDLY INTERNATIONAL

Three weeks on from the British Championship win over Wales the original tangerine wizard was back at Wembley as England faced newly crowned World Cup winners Germany. Hungary, who had hammered England twice in the previous twelve months had given the Germans the same treatment during the 1954 World Cup in a group game, winning 8 3.

When the countries met again in the final, it was the Germans who prevailed to lift their first World Cup, winning 3 2, Although only three members of the winning side were selected for this fixture, their status of World Cup winners ensured this was a massive game.

As in the game against Wales, the supply of opportunities from Matthews was frequent with Roy Bentley converting one of them to give England a half-time lead. Nineteen years on from his first encounter with the Germans Matthews produced a stirring performance on the right flank. With his great friend and rival, Tom Finney, creating a second goal early in the second half England were dominating the game to the point of overconfidence. Sloppy play allowed the Germans to pull a goal back in the seventy-seventh minutes before the Clown Prince of Sunderland, Len Shackleton scored to settle the encounter in favour of the host nation.

	1 December 1954 - **England** 3 West Germany 1	
	Player	Club
1	Ray Wood	Manchester United
2	Ron staniforth	Huddersfield Town
3	Roger Byrne	Manchester United
4	Len Phillips	Portsmouth
5	Billy Wright	Wolverhampton W
6	Bill Slater	Wolverhampton W
7	**Sranley Matthews**	**Blackpool**
8	Roy Bentley	Chelsea
9	Ronnie Allen	West Bromwich Albion
10	Len Shackleton	Sunderland
11	Tom Finney	Preston North End
	England 3 West Germany 1	

19. England v Scotland – 2 April 1955

STANLEY MATTHEWS

BRITISH CHAMPIONSHIP

With Scotland not having lost a full international at Wembley since 1934 the hope before kick-off was that Matthews and England would bring that sequence to an end. With Scotland's keeper dropping a cross to allow centre forward Dennis Wilshaw a tap in they could not have had a better start.

Six minutes later Matthews, in his fortieth year, provided the opportunity for Nat Lofthouse to double England's lead. The impact of a Scottish goal was negated by goals from Don Revie, following another goalkeeping error, and Nat Lofthouse from a clever pass by Matthews

In modern-day terminology, the key statistics of the second-half would read goals, Wilshaw 3, assists Matthews 3. Three times the wizard provided the ideal pass; each time Wolves centre forward Wilshaw applied the finish. A late Scottish goal was nothing more than a consolation as England broke the twenty-one-year sequence by thrashing their oldest rivals 7 2 with the Wizard of Dribble very much to the fore.

	2 April 1955 - **England** v Scotland	
	Player	Club
1	Bert Williams	Wolverhampton W
2	Jimmy Meadows	Manchester City
3	Roger Byrne	Manchester United
4	Ken Armstrong	Chelsea
5	Billy Wright	Wolverhampton W
6	Duncan Edwards	Manchester United
7	**Stanley Matthews**	**Blackpool**
8	Don Revie	Manchester City
9	Nat Lofthouse	Bolton Wanderers
10	Dennis Wilshaw	Wolverhampton W
11	Frank Blunstone	Chelsea
	England 7 Scotland 2	

Making his England debut that day was Manchester City right-back Jimmy Meadows who subsequently had spells as caretaker manager of the Seasiders in 1970 and again in 1978.

20. England v Northern Ireland
2 November 1955

BILL PERRY

BRITISH CHAMPIONSHIP

More than thirty years on from the first British Championship fixture to be held at Wembley, and three years on from a first visit by the Welsh, Northern Ireland visited the famous stadium for the first time. The decision to host the game at Wembley was in recognition of the seventy-fifth anniversary of the Irish FA.

Making his England debut in this fixture and becoming the ninth seasider to represent the three lions was Bill Perry, scorer of probably the most famous goal in tangerine history. Having scored four goals on his previous Wembley appearance the Wolverhampton Wanderers striker Dennis Wilshaw continued in that vein with a fifty-third-minute goal to give England the lead.

Having benefited from the wizardry of Matthews on that occasion Wilshaw was to benefit from the assistance of Perry two minutes later when heading home from his left-wing cross. An eighty-ninth-minute goal from Tom Finney sealed a comfortable win for England.

2 November 1955 - **England** v Northern Ireland	
Player	Club
1 Ron Baynam	Luton Town
2 Jeff Hall	Birmingham City
3 Roger Byrne	Manchester United
4 Ronnie Clayton	Blackburn Rovers
5 Billy Wright	Wolverhampton W
6 Jimmy Dickinson	Portsmouth
7 Tom Finney	Preston North End
8 Johnny Haynes	Fulham
9 Bernard Jezzard	Fulham
10 Dennis Wilshaw	Wolverhampton W
11 Bill Perry	**Blackpool**
England 3 Northern Ireland 0	

Tangerine trivia

Peter Doherty, manager of the Northern Irish team, made 82 appearances for Blackpool between 1933 and 1936. By winning four international caps during that period he had the distinction of being the club's most capped player. In October 1951 he became Northern Irelands first international manager guiding them to the World Cup quarter-finals in 1958.

21. England v Spain – 30 November 1955

BILL PERRY

FRIENDLY INTERNATIONAL

Four weeks on from his England debut Blackpool's goalscoring left-winger was selected to win his second cap in a friendly fixture against Spain. In doing so he would make his fourth appearance at the Empire Stadium, placing him sixth on the all-time list of appearances by Seasiders at Wembley.

In a game in which possession was equal and chance-taking was key to the outcome, the three lions got off to a flyer. The disappointment of Tom Finney missing the first-minute penalty was soon forgotten as John Atyeo of Bristol City gave England an eleventh-minute lead. Two minutes later Bill Perry became the second seasider, after Stan Mortensen , to have scored at the stadium for club and country.

As the game progressed into the second half Tom Finney atoned for his penalty miss by adding a third goal. An excellent flowing move just past the hour was finished with a firm header from Bill Perry to net his second goal of the game. A late goal for Spain was a consolation and the final whistle saw Bill Perry end his fourth Wembley appearance having scored three goals at the venue, a total bettered only by Stan Mortensen .

	30 November 1955 - England v Spain	
	Player	Club
1	Ron Baynam	Luton Town
2	Jeff Hall	Birmingham City
3	Roger Byrne	Manchester United
4	Ronnie Clayton	Blackburn Rovers
5	Billy Wright	Wolverhampton W
6	Jimmy Dickinson	Portsmouth
7	Tom Finney	Preston North End
8	John Atyeo	Bristol City
9	Nat Lofthouse	Bolton Wanderers
10	Johnny Haynes	Fulham
11	**Bill Perry**	**Blackpool**
	England 4 Spain 1	

22. England v Brazil – 29 May 1956

STANLEY MATTHEWS

FRIENDLY INTERNATIONAL

The forty-one-year-old wizard of dribble was back at the Empire Stadium for his eleventh appearance as a seasider for the first international fixture played on these shores against a Brazil developing into one of the all-time great national teams. Brazil were building towards the 1958 World Cup in Sweden in which they would claim the Jules Rimet Trophy for the first time.

Match reports of the time suggest this game was one of the finest ever seen at the stadium and there is little doubt Matthews performance was one of his best, for club or country. Having seen a first-minute penalty missed by England he participated in flowing moves that saw the ball end up in the Brazilian net twice inside the first five minutes courtesy of Tommy Taylor and debutant Colin Grainger. An enthralling game developed as opportunities came and went at both ends in a half that finished with England leading 2 0.

Within ten minutes of the restart, Brazil had levelled the scores at 2 2 as a match described as breathless continued to ebb and flow. Matthews continued to menace the Brazilian defence and with sixty-seven minutes on the clock, his right-wing cross lead to Manchester United's Tommy Taylor scoring his second goal of the game to restore England's lead. A minute later England were awarded a second penalty which, like the first, was missed.

As England edged towards a win an eighty-fourth minute cross from Matthews was headed home by Grainger of Sheffield United for his second goal of the game, ultimately settling a terrific game of football in favour of the three lions.

	9 May 1956 - **England** v Brazil	
	Player	Club
1	Reg Matthews	Coventry City
2	Jeff Hall	Birmingham City
3	Roger Byrne	Manchester United
4	Ronnie Clayton	Blackburn Rovers
5	Billy Wright	Wolverhampton W
6	Duncan Edwards	Manchester United
7	**Stanley Matthews**	**Blackpool**
8	John Atyeo	Bristol City
9	Tommy Taylor	Manchester United
10	Johnny Haynes	Fulham
11	Colin Grainger	Sheffield United
	England 4 Brazil 2	

Three Lions Trivia

Joining the Wizard of Dribble for one of his finest performances was an artist with experience of a different stage. Known as the Singing Winger, in his alternate occupation as a professional singer Colin Grainger shared the bill with the Beatles at a show in Stockport .

23. England v Wales - 14 November 1956

STANLEY MATTHEWS

BRITISH CHAMPIONSHIP

With England now playing all their home fixtures in the British Championship at Wembley the second visit of the Welsh saw Matthews make his twelfth appearance at the stadium as a seasider.

Although the wizard was as prominent as ever in an England shirt the games major talking point was that substitutes were not yet a regular feature. That Wales lost their keeper to injury early in the game and both teams finished with ten players clearly impacted the game and possibly the outcome.

For Wales, the delight of a fourteenth-minute goal for John Charles became disappointment a minute later when keeper Jack Kelsey was injured bravely diving at the feet of Tom Finney. Despite being down to ten men for the remainder of the game, and down to nine for a short time, the Welsh showed great resolve in holding out until the forty-eighth minute when Johnny Haynes of Fulham equalised.

Three minutes later debutant Johnny Brooks of Tottenham Hotspur latched on to Matthews through ball to give England the lead. The outcome was settled when a right-wing cross from the wizard of dribble was converted by the Preston Plumber, Tom Finney.

	14 November 1956 - **England** v Wales	
	Player	Club
1	Ted Ditchburn	Tottenham Hotspur
2	Jeff Hall	Birmingham City
3	Roger Byrne	Manchester United
4	Ronnie Clayton	Blackburn Rovers
5	Billy Wright	Wolverhampton W
6	Jimmy Dickinson	Portsmouth
7	**Stanley Matthews**	**Blackpool**
8	John Brooks	Tottenham Hotspur
9	Tom Finney	Preston North End
10	Johnny Haynes	Fulham
11	Colin Grainger	Sheffield United
	England 3 Wales 1	

24. England v Yugoslavia - 28 November 1956

STANLEY MATTHEWS

FRIENDLY INTERNATIONAL

Stans thirteenth appearance at the Empire Stadium while employed by Blackpool Football Club was unlucky for Yugoslavia and left back Branko Stankovic. At one point he resorted to a tackle on the wizard that prompted Matthews to question whether the game belonged at Twickenham rather than Wembley.

Winning his fiftieth cap in total Stan participated in the build-up to John Brook's opening goal in the twelfth minute. By contrast to the British Championship, the pre-match agreement between the countries was that substitutes would be allowed for injury before the forty-fourth minute. With thirty-five minutes gone Fulham's Johnny Haynes was unable to continue following injury and Tommy Taylor of Manchester United became the first player to be introduced by England as a substitute at Wembley.

With Matthews and Finney in full flight, the Yugoslav keeper Vladimir Beara was kept busy. When Taylor added a second goal in the fifty-eighth minute the floodgates would have opened had it not been for Beara. On the hour Stankovic conceded a penalty for a challenge on Matthews. With the spot kick missed the disappointment eased in the penultimate minute of the game when Matthews provided the opportunity for Taylor to score his second and England's third goal of the afternoon.

	28 November 1956 - **England** v Yugoslavia	
	Player	Club
1	Ted Ditchburn	Tottenham Hotspur
2	Jeff Hall	Birmingham City
3	Roger Byrne	Manchester United
4	Ronnie Clayton	Blackburn Rovers
5	Billy Wright	Wolverhampton W
6	Jimmy Dickinson	Portsmouth
7	**Stanley Matthews**	**Blackpool**
8	John Brooks	Tottenham Hotspur
9	Tom Finney	Preston North End
10	Johnny Haynes	Fulham
11	Frank Blunstone	Chelsea
	England 3 Yugoslavia 0	

25. England v Scotland – 6 April 1957

STANLEY MATTHEWS - ENGLAND
JACKIE MUDIE - SCOTLAND

BRITISH CHAMPIONSHIP

The decisive fixture in the 1957 British Championship generated another first for Blackpool Football Club. With forty-two-year-old Stanley Matthews making his fourteenth Wembley appearance as a seasider and Jackie Mudie making his third appearance it was the first time two Blackpool players had been in opposition in a full international fixture.

Both countries had taken three points from their fixtures against Wales and Northern Ireland and both Blackpool forwards were making their third championship appearance of the season.

With two minutes gone it was Scotland who held the advantage when left winger Tommy Ring of Clyde intercepted a pass intended for Matthews and went through to score. The visitors, with Mudie to the fore, were the better side in the early exchanges and held the lead for an hour before West Bromwich Albion's debutant forward Derek Kevan equalised to keep the destination of the British Championship trophy in the balance.

As had happened so many times throughout his previous fifty-one appearances for the three lions Matthews was involved in the decisive moments as he dribbled past two defenders and squared the ball for Duncan Edwards of Manchester United to drill home the eighty-fourth minute winning goal and secure a sixth consecutive British Championship title for England.

Tangerine Trivia

Away from the international arena Matthews and Mudie were colleagues for a large part of their footballing career. After leaving Blackpool the pair linked up at Stoke City helping them to win the second division title in the 1962-3 season.

	6 April 1957 - England v Scotland	
	England	
	Player	Club
1	Alan Hodgkinson	Sheffield United
2	Jeff Hall	Birmingham City
3	Roger Byrne	Manchester United
4	Ronnie Clayton	Blackburn Rovers
5	Billy Wright	Wolverhampton W
6	Duncan Edwards	Manchester United
7	**Stanley Matthews**	**Blackpool**
8	Thomas Thompson	Preston North End
9	Tom Finney	Preston North End
10	Derek Kevan	West Bromwich Albiion
11	Colin Grainger	Sunderland
	Scotland	
	Player	Club
1	Tom Younger	Hibernian
2	Eric Caldow	Rangers
3	John Hewie	Charlton Athletic
4	John McColl	Rangers
5	George Young	Rangers
6	Tommy Docherty	Preston North End
7	Bobby Collins	Celtic
8	Will Fernie	Celtic
9	Lawrie Reilly	Hibernian
10	**Jackie Mudie**	**Blackpool**
11	Tommy Ring	Clyde
	England 2 Scotland 1	

26. England v Republic of Ireland - 8 May 1957

STANLEY MATTHEWS

WORLD CUP QUALIFICATION MATCH UEFA GROUP 1

A month on from the British Championship decider against Scotland the tangerine wizard of dribble was back at the Empire Stadium to earn his fifty-third England cap and make his fifteenth and final appearance as a Seasider at a venue where he had entertained supporters and demoralised opponents in equal measure.

Although this was England's third World Cup qualifying campaign it was the first such fixture to be played at the Empire Stadium. The first time the home nations entered the World Cup was for the 1950 tournament to be held in Brazil. FIFA determined qualification places would be available to the nations placed first and second in the 1949-50 British Championship.

The same criterion was applied for the 1954 World Cup in Switzerland with the 1953-54 British Championship doubling up to determine which two nations would qualify. In both the 1949-50 and 1953-54 seasons England travelled to Wales and Scotland while Northern Ireland was hosted in the North of the country. Recognising this format guaranteed the home nations two qualifying places the process was revised. The outcome was all four home nations were drawn into separate groups.

England were drawn in UEFA Group 1 alongside Denmark and Ireland. Matthews had played his part in helping England to a 5 2 win over Denmark in their opening fixture with Manchester United centre forward Tommy Taylor netting a hat trick. Against the Irish, England, with Matthews to the fore, stormed out of the blocks to lead 4 0 at half-time with Tommy Taylor netting a second consecutive hat trick and Bristol City's John Atyeo finding the target. A second goal from Atyeo early in the second half and a late consolation goal for the Irish concluded the scoring and left England top of the group.

8 May 1957 - **England** v Republic of Ireland		
	Player	Club
1	Alan Hodgkinson	Sheffield United
2	Jeff Hall	Birmingham City
3	Roger Byrne	Manchester United
4	Ronnie Clayton	Blackburn Rovers
5	Billy Wright	Wolverhampton W
6	Duncan Edwards	Manchester United
7	**Stanley Matthews**	**Blackpool**
8	John Atyeo	Bristol City
9	Tommy Taylor	Manchester United
10	Johnny Haynes	Fulham
11	Tom Finney	Preston North End
England 5 Republic of Ireland 1		

Three Lions trivia

One week on from his final appearance at the Empire Stadium Matthews, often known as Mr Football, was to make fifty-fourth and final appearance in an England shirt. At the age of forty-two and twenty-two years after his debut, he was selected for the World Cup qualifying fixture in Denmark on 15 May and played his part in a 4 1 win. Injury prevented selection for the final qualifying fixture in Ireland four days later and, although it was not known at the time, his time as an England international was at an end.

Tangerine Trivia

Selection for the game in Denmark earned Matthews his thirty-sixth England cap during his time with the Seasiders earning him the distinction of being Blackpool's most capped player until his total was passed by another tangerine legend, Jimmy Armfield. Also included in the England squad for this fixture was Roy Gratrix who had established himself as the Seasiders centre half following the retirement of Harry Johnston. Consistent performances for the club brought him into contention for an England place but unfortunately, not into the team.

27. England v Rumania - 16 October 1957

JIMMY ARMFIELD

UNDER 23 FRIENDLY INTERNATIONAL

Having broken into a Blackpool team that finished runners-up to Matt Busby's Manchester United side in the 1955-56 season and just five months after Stanley Matthews club record fifteenth Wembley appearance a promising young full-back by the name of Jimmy Armfield made his first at the Stadium in a landmark fixture. The game against Rumania was the first under 23 international fixture to be played at Wembley.

Also making his Wembley debut in this game was a young striker by the name of Jimmy Greaves who scored twice in the first twenty minutes to put England in charge. Not being over-awed the Rumanians levelled the scores by half-time. The only goal of the second half went England's way to earn the young Lions a 3 2 win in the first of many Wembley appearances for these two emerging talents in the English game.

	16 October 1957 - **England U23** v Rumania U23	
	Player	Club
1	Alan Hodgkinson	Sheffield United
2	**Jimmy Armfield**	**Blackpool**
3	Gerry Harris	Wolverhampton W
4	Maurice Setters	West Bromwich Albion
5	Trevor Smith	Birmingham City
6	Stan Crowther	Aston Villa
7	Peter Brabrook	Chelsea
8	Jimmy Greaves	Chelsea
9	Billy Curry	Newcastle United
10	Ray Parry	Bolton Wanderers
11	Alan A'Court	Liverpool
	England 3 Rumania 2	

Three Lions trivia

Along with Ray Parry, Jim was originally selected as a reserve for this game. In the event both players made their Wembley debuts. The pair subsequently lined up together for the senior team at Hampden Park in April 1960. Six months later they became teammates at Bloomfield Road,

28. England v Yugoslavia - 11 May 1960

JIMMY ARMFIELD

FRIENDLY INTERNATIONAL

Following Stanley Matthews final Wembley appearance against Ireland in May 1957 the next seasider to feature at the famous stadium in a full international was the man who went on to make over 600 appearances for the Pool and become their most capped player, Jimmy Armfield.

By the time gentleman Jim was selected for this fixture he already made his Wembley debut and been capped five times for his country, the first four of which were earned playing at left-back. Having already played in front of crowds exceeding 100,000 in the Maracanã Stadium in Brazil, and at Hampden Park against Scotland, a full international appearance at Wembley was unlikely to faze him.

With Jim starting in his accustomed right-back position for the second time it was clear the three lions would have a difficult match against a talented side when Milan Gallic gave the visitors an early lead. England hit back with goals from Bryan Douglas and Jimmy Greaves to lead 2 1 at half-time.

A second goal from Gallic and an eightieth-minute strike from Bora Kostic put former Yugoslavia on the verge of a first win on English soil. As the game moved into the final 90 seconds England produced a stirring finish as centre forward Joe Baker twice hit the crossbar with thumping headers. On the first occasion, Johnny Haynes was on hand to net the rebound to level the scores. From the second rebound, no one was on hand to capitalise, and an excellent game ended in a 3 3 draw.

11 May 1960 - England v Yugoslavia	
Player	Club
Ron Springett	Sheffield Wednesday
Jimmy Armfield	**Blackpool**
Ray Wilson	Huddersfield Town
Ronnie Clayton	Blackburn Rovers
Peter Swan	Sheffield Wednesday
Ron Flowers	Wolverhampton W
Bryan Douglas	Blackburn Rovers
Johnny Haynes	Fulham
Joe Baker	Hibernian
Jimmy Greaves	Chelsea
Bobby Charlton	Manchester United
England 3 Yugoslavia 3	

29. England v Spain - 26 October 1960

JIMMY ARMFIELD

FRIENDLY INTERNATIONAL

In an era when the primary role of a right-back was to mark and nullify the threat of the opposition left winger Jimmy Armfield was a revelation for club and country. Blessed with natural pace he was able to overlap players ahead of him and bring another dimension to forward play without detriment to his defensive duties.

As the England manager, Walter Winterbottom sought to bring consistency of selection and performance to the side as they looked to qualify and build for the 1962 World Cup in Chile, it was clear Jim was a player who met the requirements.

His direct opponent for his second Wembley appearance was Francisco Gento Lopez, a member of the Real Madrid side winning five consecutive European Cups from 1956 to 1960. Media reports of the rain-sodden game confirm an enthralling individual contest between Armfield and Gento was a pivotal factor in the outcome of the match.

A first-minute goal from Jimmy Greaves saw England off to a flyer only for Luis Del Sol to equalise for Spain ten minutes later. As half-time approached Bryan Douglas of Blackburn Rovers, found the net to restore the lead for the three lions. A lively start to the second half saw Luis Suarez of Barcelona equalise for the second time,

In a delicately balanced game Bobby Smith, who had scored on each of his first two England appearances put them ahead for the third time on the hour with a well-judged chip from just outside the penalty area. With Armfield keeping a tight rein on the dangerous Gento and supporting the attack England finished strongly with Smith scoring his second goal of the game to secure a 4-2 win.

26 October 1960 - England v Spain		
	Player	Club
1	Ron Springett	Sheffield Wednesday
2	**Jimmy Armfield**	**Blackpool**
3	Micheal McNeil	Middlesbrough
4	Bobby Robson	West Bromwich Albion
5	Peter Swan	Sheffield Wednesday
6	Ron Flowers	Wolverhampton W
7	Bryan Douglas	Blackburn Rovers
8	Jimmy Greaves	Chelsea
9	Bobby Smith	Tottenham Hotspur
10	Johnny Haynes	Fulham
11	Bobby Charlton	Manchester United
England 4 Spain 2		

Tangerine trivia

Scorer of Spain's second, goal and known as the architect for his vision and skill on a football pitch, Luis Suarez won many accolades and honours during his career. In 1960, he became the first Spaniard to win the Balon D'Or. On 7 June 1972, he became the first overseas winner of the Balon D'or to grace the Bloomfield Road pitch when playing for Sampdoria in the Anglo-Italian Cup.

30. England v Wales - 23 November 1960

JIMMY ARMFIELD

BRITISH CHAMPIONSHIP

A month on from his outstanding dual with Real Madrid winger Gento Jim again would need to be on his mettle against the Tottenham Hotspur left-winger Cliff Jones, a player who made a huge contribution to the double-winning team of 1960-61 and beyond.

Once again, England were quickly out of the traps as goals from Greaves, Bobby Charlton and Bobby Smith had them 3 0 up after 22 minutes. Second-half goals from Greaves and captain Johnny Haynes continued a goal-laden international season before a late Welsh consolation goal completed the scoring

	23 November 1960 - **England** v Wales	
	Player	Club
1	Alan Hodgkinson	Sheffield United
2	**Jimmy Armfield**	**Blackpool**
3	Micheal McNeil	Middlesbrough
4	Bobby Robson	West Bromwich Albion
5	Peter Swan	Sheffield Wednesday
6	Ron Flowers	Wolverhampton W
7	Bryan Douglas	Blackburn Rovers
8	Jimmy Greaves	Chelsea
9	Bobby Smith	Tottenham Hotspur
10	Johnny Haynes	Fulham
11	Bobby Charlton	Manchester United
	England 5 Wales 1	

31. England v Scotland – 15 April 1961

JIMMY ARMFIELD

BRITISH CHAMPIONSHIP

With 10 goals in the British Championship fixtures against Northern Ireland and Wales, an unchanged England side were looking to maintain their goalscoring habits against Scotland. Jim's direct opponent for this fixture was Davie Wilson of Glasgow Rangers who played his part in helping his club win the league title in Scotland and become the first British club to reach the final of a European competition.

Once again England started strongly with a goal from Bobby Robson and two from Jimmy Greaves to lead 3 0 at half-time. Within ten minutes of the restart, a thunderous drive from another of Tottenham's 1960-61 double winners, Dave Mackay, and a header from Jim's direct opponent Davie Wilson had found the back of the English net to keep Scotland very much in the game at 3 2
.

The fourth goal for England, scored by Bryan Douglas, was countered by a goal from debutant Pat Quinn for Scotland. With fifteen minutes left England led 4 3 and a nail-biting finish to the game was on the cards. Ten minutes later, with captain Johnny Haynes pulling the strings, England led by 9 goals to 3. With Bobby Smith and the captain each scoring twice and Greaves completing his hat trick the Scots were in danger of conceding double figures before the referees' whistle confirmed England as British champions.

	15 April 1961 - **England** v Scotland	
	Player	Club
1	Ron Springett	Sheffield Wednesday
2	**Jimmy Armfield**	**Blackpool**
3	Micheal McNeil	Middlesbrough
4	Bobby Robson	West Bromwich Albion
5	Peter Swan	Sheffield Wednesday
6	Ron Flowers	Wolverhampton W
7	Bryan Douglas	Blackburn Rovers
8	Jimmy Greaves	Chelsea
9	Bobby Smith	Tottenham Hotspur
10	Johnny Haynes	Fulham
11	Bobby Charlton	Manchester United
	England 9 Scotland 3	

Tangerine Trivia

There is doubt over the scorer of the third Scottish goal. Some match reports and newsreel credit the goal as a second for Davie Wilson of Rangers, who was Jimmy Armfield's direct opponent while other sources credit the goal to debutant Pat Quinn who subsequently signed for Blackpool.

32. England v Mexico – 10 May 1961

JIMMY ARMFIELD

FRIENDLY INTERNATIONAL

Just under a month on from the demolition of the auld enemy gentlemen Jim was making his fifth Wembley appearance and winning his fourteenth cap in total. Injury and suspension deprived England of the services of Jimmy Greaves and Bobby Smith who had scored five goals between them in the win over Scotland.

The remainder of the team was unchanged and unaffected by their absence as debutant Gerry Hitchens gave England a first-minute lead. By the time the game had reached the twenty-third minute two goals from Bobby Charlton and one from Bobby Robson had England in complete control of their destiny. A fifth goal from Bryan Douglas completed a miserable first half for the visitors and ensured damage limitation was the order of the day.

With Ron Flowers converting a penalty and Bobby Charlton completing a hat trick England lead 7 0 with thirty minutes to go. For the second match running double figures was a possibility for the three lions. Although chances continued to be made only one of them was taken, by Bryan Douglas, in the eighty-fifth minute. With a three-match European tour to follow, including a World Cup qualifying fixture, England, with forty goals in their previous six internationals, were in good form.

10 May 1961 - **England** v Mexico		
	Player	Club
1	Ron Springett	Sheffield Wednesday
2	**Jimmy Armfield**	**Blackpool**
3	Micheal McNeil	Middlesbrough
4	Bobby Robson	West Bromwich Albion
5	Peter Swan	Sheffield Wednesday
6	Ron Flowers	Wolverhampton W
7	Bryan Douglas	Blackburn Rovers
8	Derek Kevan	West Bromwich Albion
9	Gerry Hitchens	Aston Villa
10	Johnny Haynes	Fulham
11	Bobby Charlton	Manchester United
England 8 Mexico 0		

33. England v Portugal – 25 October 1961

JIMMY ARMFIELD

WORLD CUP QUALIFICATION - UEFA GROUP 6

By the time of his sixth Wembley appearance, Jimmy Armfield had another personal milestone worthy of recording in the tangerine record books and England was in the driving seat in terms of World Cup qualification.

Drawn in UEFA group 6 alongside Luxembourg and Portugal England had opened their qualifying campaign by winning 9 0 in the Grand Duchy in October 1960. Having then opened their three-match European tour with a hard-earned draw in Lisbon against a side containing several players from the Benfica side that was an emerging European force England, with two home games to come, were well placed to qualify.

Although not played at Wembley the home fixture against Luxembourg is worthy of mention. With Johnny Haynes injured Jim was afforded the honour of captaining his country for the first time. Although not a great game, a 4-1 win put England on the brink of qualification.

Having used just fourteen players in the nine-game 1960-61 season, coach Walter Winterbottom had used that many in the first two games of the 1961-62 international season. With Portugal needing a win they were given a mountain to climb as two members of Burnley's 1959-60 League Championship winning side, John Connelly and Ray Pointer, found the net in the fifth and ninth minutes, respectively.

The rising star of the world game, Eusebio, threatened in the closing stages but England saw the game out to claim first place in the three-team group. Although England had qualified for the World Cup finals the goal-laden power and fluency of the previous season had been lost.

	25 October 1961 - **England** v Portugal	
	Player	Club
1	Ron Springett	Sheffield Wednesday
2	**Jimmy Armfield**	**Blackpool**
3	Ray Wilson	Huddersfield Town
4	Bobby Robson	West Bromwich Albion
5	Peter Swan	Sheffield Wednesday
6	Ron Flowers	Wolverhampton W
7	John Connelly	Burnley
8	Bryan Douglas	Blackburn Rovers
9	Ray Pointer	Burnley
10	Johnny Haynes	Fulham
11	Bobby Charlton	Manchester United
	England 2 Portugal 0	

34. England v Northern Ireland
22 November 1961

JIMMY ARMFIELD

BRITISH CHAMPIONSHIP

Following on from the World Cup qualifier against Portugal selection for the British Championship fixture against Northern Ireland moved Jim into outright third place behind Matthews and Mortensen on the Wembley Seasiders appearance list.

After the consistency of selection and performance achieved the previous season, the game was attended by a then record low crowd of 30,000 for an England game at Wembley. Bobby Charlton's first-half goal was equalised by Jimmy McIlroy in the closing stages as the game finished all square.

	22 November 1961 - **England** v Northern Ireland		
	Player	Club	
1	Ron Springett	Sheffield Wednesday	
2	**Jimmy Armfield**	**Blackpool**	
3	Ray Wilson	Huddersfield Town	
4	Bobby Robson	West Bromwich Albion	
5	Peter Swan	Sheffield Wednesday	
6	Ron Flowers	Wolverhampton W	
7	Bryan Douglas	Blackburn Rovers	
8	John Byrne	Crystal Palace	
9	Ray Crawford	Ipswich Town	
10	Johnny Haynes	Fulham	
11	Bobby Charlton	Manchester United	
	England 1 Northern Ireland 1		

35. England v Austria - 4 April 1962

JIMMY ARMFIELD

FRIENDLY INTERNATIONAL

Selection for his eighth Wembley appearance earned Jim his twenty-second England cap. With only three members of the teams having more caps than Jim and five in single fingers it was clear there was no certainty as to who would go to the world cup in Chile. An early goal from Ray Crawford and a thirty-seventh-minute penalty from Ron Flowers saw the Lions in control by half time. A debut goal from Roger Hunt in the sixty-seventh minute and an Austrian goal ten minutes later completed the scoring.

In the submission of a preliminary 40 player squad on 10 April, the players selected for this match were clear candidates for a place in the squad. On the 15 April, the final squad of 22 was announced. Of the 11 players selected for this game only 1, the Ipswich Town centre-forward Ray Crawford, wasn't selected. For gentlemen Jim selection was to be a true career highlight as his consistent performance ensured he was considered "world class" by the media.

	4 April 1962 - **England** v Austria	
	Player	Club
1	Ron Springett	Sheffield Wednesday
2	**Jimmy Armfield**	**Blackpool**
3	Ray Wilson	Huddersfield Town
4	Stan Anderson	Middlesbrough
5	Peter Swan	Sheffield Wednesday
6	Ron Flowers	Wolverhampton W
7	John Connelly	Burnley
8	Roger Hunt	Liverpool
9	Ray Crawford	Ipswich Town
10	Johnny Haynes	Fulham
11	Bobby Charlton	Manchester United
	England 3 Austria 1	

36. England v Switzerland - 9 May 1962

JIMMY ARMFIELD

FRIENDLY INTERNATIONAL

England's final international before departing for the World Cup in Chile saw Jim make his ninth Wembley appearance against fellow finalists Switzerland. With first half goals from Ron Flowers, Gerry Hitchens and John Connolly against one from the Swiss England were perceived to be in charge.

With the Swiss dominating the second half the combination of a stubborn England defence and an inspired performance from goalkeeper Ron Springett was needed before the final whistle confirmed England would leave for the world cup with a win and give Gentlemen Jim and his team mates the opportunity to test themselves against some of the world's finest national teams.

	9 May 1962 - **England** v Switzerland	
	Player	Club
1	Ron Springett	Sheffield Wednesday
2	**Jimmy Armfield**	**Blackpool**
3	Ray Wilson	Huddersfield Town
4	Bobby Robson	West Bromwich Albion
5	Peter Swan	Sheffield Wednesday
6	Ron Flowers	Wolverhampton W
7	John Connelly	Burnley
8	Jimmy Greaves	Tottenham Hotspur
9	Gerry Hitchens	Inter Milan
10	Johnny Haynes	Fulham
11	Bobby Charlton	Manchester United
	England 3 Switzerland 1	

37. England v Wales - 21 November 1962

JIMMY ARMFIELD

BRITISH CHAMPIONSHIP

By the time of Jim's tenth Wembley appearance, his status within the game was clear. His performances at the World Cup in Chile saw him regarded by many as the best right-back in the world. When returning to international football for the European Nations Cup first leg tie against France he was named captain of England for the second time.

Hence, in his tenth Wembley appearance gentlemen, Jimmy Armfield would lead the team out at the stadium for the first time. With five players who played in the world cup quarter-final against Brazil missing from Walter Winterbottom's final match as manager England started well. A seventh-minute goal from John Connolly and goals from Middlesbrough centre forward Alan Peacock in the thirty-fifth and sixty-third minutes put England in control.

A goal from Jimmy Greaves with two minutes left completed the scoring and Walter Winterbottom's final match as England manager had ended with a convincing win. In his role as captain Jim presented the retiring manager with a set of crystal goblets.

With thirty-two caps and now four-time captain of England, the standing of Jimmy Armfield as one of Blackpool and England's greatest players was not in doubt. The question now was would the incoming England manager, Alf Ramsey, agree?

21 November 1962 - **England** v Wales	
Player	Club
1 Ron Springett	Sheffield Wednesday
2 **Jimmy Armfield**	**Blackpool**
3 Graham Shaw	Sheffield United
4 Bobby Moore	West Ham United
5 Brian Labone	Everton
6 Ron Flowers	Wolverhampton W
7 John Connelly	Burnley
8 Freddie Hill	Bolton Wanderers
9 Alan Peacock	Middlesbrough
10 Jimmy Greaves	Tottenham Hotspur
11 Bobby Tambling	Chelsea
England 4 Wales 0	

38. England v Scotland – 6 April 1963

JIMMY ARMFIELD

BRITISH CHAMPIONSHIP

Alf Ramsey's first game as England manager, the second leg of the European Nations Cup tie against France had not gone well. Beaten 5 2 England had lost the tie 6 3 on an aggregate score. The focus would turn to the 1966 World Cup which would be held in England. With Jimmy Armfield retaining the captaincy he was surely going to be a contender for the final squad and the captaincy.

The opposition for Ramsey's Wembley debut as England manager was the auld enemy who, having been thrashed 9 3 on their last visit sought redemption. Making his eleventh Wembley appearance, Jim's direct opponent once again was Davie Wilson of Glasgow Rangers. A fifth-minute collision between the England centre-forward, Bobby Smith, and Scotland defender Eric Caldow saw both teams reduced to ten men. With the use of substitutes still not an option in competitive fixtures a reshuffle of resources was required.

With Caldow suffering a serious injury he was not able to return while Bobby Smith came out for the second half and remained on the right-wing to add 'nuisance value." By the time he returned Scotland were in control of their destiny. The maverick Jim Baxter was turning in a command performance to drive his team to victory. With twenty-nine minutes on the clock, he dispossessed a hesitant Jimmy Armfield in the England penalty area and drilled a shot beyond debutant keeper Gordon Banks to put Scotland in front.

Minutes later Baxter was brought down in the area to gain the Scots a penalty kick which he converted himself. Although Bobby Smith returned after halftime to give England a numerical advantage, he was restricted by injury. A goal from Bryan Douglas with ten minutes to go gave the Lions hope but the Scots saw the game out to register another Wembley triumph and retain the British Championship for a second season running.

	6 April 1963 - **England** v Scotland	
	Player	Club
1	Gordon Banks	Leicester City
2	**Jimmy Armfield**	**Blackpool**
3	Gerry Byrne	Liverpool
4	Bobby Moore	West Ham United
5	Maurice Norman	Tottenham Hotspur
6	Ron Flowers	Wolverhampton W
7	Bryan Douglas	Blackburn Rovers
8	Jimmy Greaves	Tottenham Hotspur
9	Bobby Smith	Tottenham Hotspur
10	Jimmy Melia	Liverpool
11	Bobby Charlton	Manchester United
	England 1 Scotland 2	

39. England v Brazil - 8 May 1963

JIMMY ARMFIELD

FA CENTENARY CELEBRATION MATCH

For Jim's seventh match as England captain and Alf Ramsey's third as England manager, the visitors to Wembley were the reigning World Cup Holders, Brazil. In a team where Bobby Charlton, winning his forty-second cap, was the most capped England player on view the structure of Ramsey's side was beginning to take shape. Seven of the starting eleven would feature in the twenty-two-player squad for the 1966 World Cup.

A piece of Brazilian magic gave the visitors the advantage when Pepe scored from a twenty-fifth-minute free-kick that allegedly swerved like a banana in flight. With a third straight defeat in sight for Ramsey, a shot from Jim was diverted by Bobby Charlton into the path of Bryan Douglas to net an eighty-fifth-minute equaliser to earn England an encouraging result.

	8 May 1963 - **England** v Brazil	
	Player	Club
1	Gordon Banks	Leicester City
2	**Jimmy Armfield**	**Blackpool**
3	Ray Wilson	huddersfield Town
4	Gordon Milne	Liverpool
5	Maurice Norman	Tottenham Hotspur
6	Bobby Moore	West Ham United
7	Bryan Douglas	Blackburn Rovers
8	Jimmy Greaves	Tottenham Hotspur
9	Bobby Smith	Tottenham Hotspur
10	George Eastham	Arsenal
11	Bobby Charlton	Manchester United
	England 1 Brazil 1	

Three Lions Trivia

The two England debutants in this fixture, Gordon Milne of Liverpool and George Eastham of Stoke City both had Blackpool connections. Having helped Liverpool win the league title in 1966 Gordon Milne signed for Blackpool in May 1967. George Eastham never wore the tangerine shirt; he was simply born in the seaside resort.

40. England v Rest of the Word
23 October 1963

JIMMY ARMFIELD

FA CENTENARY CELEBRATION MATCH

In the time this prestigious game took place Ramsey, with Jimmy Armfield as captain, had taken full responsibility for team selection and could now develop the team he wanted to play without any perceived interference. By the time of the next Wembley fixture England had recorded four consecutive wins away from home and Jimmy Armfield had passed Stanley Matthews tally of thirty-six international appearances to become Blackpool's most capped international footballer.

To celebrate the Centenary of the formation of the Football Association England were to face a Rest of the World side for the second time. As in the first fixture, ten years previously, Blackpool Football Club would be represented by one of their greatest ever players. That the cover picture of his autobiography, Right Back to the Beginning, features Jim leading England out alongside the Rest of the World captain, Alfredo de Stefano, indicates the prestige he attached to this fixture.

With six players in the sixteen player Rest of the World squad who earned the title of European Footballer of the Year at some point in their careers the talent in the opposing side was immense. The highlight of the first half was the "duel" between Jimmy Greaves and the Rest of the World keeper, Lev Yashin. Three times Greaves appeared certain to score and three times he was denied by a keeper recognised as one of the greatest of all time.

Jim's individual challenge, in his thirteenth Wembley appearance, was to keep the then five-time European Cup Winner Francisco Gento, of Real Madrid and Spain, in check. With Yashin replaced at halftime England took the lead in the seventieth minute with a goal from Southampton's Terry Paine, only for Scotland's Denis Law to equalise twelve minutes later. With three minutes remaining Greaves finally earned a reward for a terrific individual performance when he netted the winning goal.

23 October 1963 - **England** v Rest of the World		
	Player	Club
1	Gordon Banks	Leicester City
2	**Jimmy Armfield**	**Blackpool**
3	Ray Wilson	huddersfield Town
4	Gordon Milne	Liverpool
5	Maurice Norman	Tottenham Hotspur
6	Bobby Moore	West Ham United
7	Terry Paine	Southampton
8	Jimmy Greaves	Tottenham Hotspur
9	Bobby Smith	Tottenham Hotspur
10	George Eastham	Arsenal
11	Bobby Charlton	Manchester United
	England 2 Rest of the World 1	

Three Lions Trivia

As with the first game in 1953, FIFA elected not to recognise the fixture as a full international. With England facing a team made up of sixteen of the World's finest players the FA thought otherwise, and the players retained their "caps" for the fixture.

41. England v Northern Ireland
20 November 1963

JIMMY ARMFIELD

BRITISH CHAMPIONSHIP

Four weeks on from facing the challenge presented by some of the world's finest footballers Jim made his fourteenth Wembley appearance. With Blackpool's finest full-back captaining his country for the twelfth time a rampant England team lead 4 0 after thirty-seven minutes when Terry Paine netted his second goal. With Paine's two goals having been separated by two from Jimmy Greaves a Johnny Crossan goal on the stroke of halftime for a reeling Irish side reminded everyone they were still in the game.

England stormed out of the blocks in the second half as Tottenham centre forward Bobby Smith netted his thirteenth goal for his country in what turned out to be his final appearance. Goals in the sixtieth minute from Paine and sixty-first minute from Greaves saw them complete their respective hat tricks.

A fourth goal for Greaves in the sixty-seventh minute meant, not for the first time in Jim's England career, double figures were possible. As they had done in the first half the Irish rallied, with Falkirk centre forward Sammy Wilson scoring twice in the closing stages to provide some consolation. The referee's whistle concluded Jim's fortieth appearance for England and what turned out to be his penultimate Wembley appearance.

20 November 1963 - **England** v Northern Ireland		
	Player	Club
1	Gordon Banks	Leicester City
2	**Jimmy Armfield**	**Blackpool**
3	Bobby Thomson	Wolverhampton W
4	Gordon Milne	Liverpool
5	Maurice Norman	Tottenham Hotspur
6	Bobby Moore	West Ham United
7	Terry Paine	Southampton
8	Jimmy Greaves	Tottenham Hotspur
9	Bobby Smith	Tottenham Hotspur
10	George Eastham	Arsenal
11	Bobby Charlton	Manchester United
England 8 Northern Ireland 3		

What happened next?

When Jimmy Armfield missed a game against the 1962 World Cup finalists Czechoslovakia he was replaced as captain by Bobby Moore. When returning to the side Jim did so as captain. Having become Blackpool's most capped player and the first seasider to reach the milestone of forty international caps he earned his forty-first cap in the British Championship decider against Scotland at Hampden Park.

Injury received In Blackpool's final league game of the season against Wolverhampton Wanderers at Molineux ruled Jim out of the Wembley friendly against Uruguay and the summer tour fixtures. Replacing Jim as captain for the second time was Bobby Moore and making his debut at right-back was George Cohen of Fulham. With Gordon Banks in goal and Ray Wilson at left-back, four members of England's World Cup-winning defence were playing together for the first time.

42. England v Belgium - 21 October 1964

TONY WAITERS

INTERNATIONAL FRIENDLY

With England qualifying as hosts for the 1966 World Cup selection suggested Alf Ramsey was experimenting as he looked to form his twenty-two-player squad. Having been included in seven England squads and selected twice it was clear Alf Ramsey was having a good look at Blackpool's Tony Waiters as one of his goalkeeping options.

Selection against Belgium meant a third cap and a Wembley debut for Waiters in an experimental England side. The Belgians, by comparison, had a settled side including eight players from Anderlecht, the reigning league champions.

With twenty-two minutes on the clock the Belgians, having been denied on more than one occasion by Waiters, took the lead when Jean Cornell's gave him no chance. Ten minutes later, a future tangerine legend, Fred Pickering, equalised for the three lions. With halftime approaching Paul Van Himst, one of Belgium's greatest players restored the visitors lead courtesy of a huge deflection.

With the settled Belgian side looking the better team England had a large slice of luck in the seventieth minute when a left-wing cross from Alan Hinton was deflected into the Belgian net to level the scores and prevent the visitors from becoming only the third overseas nation to win at Wembley.

21 October 1964 - **England** v Belgium	
Player	Club
1 **Tony Waiters**	**Blackpool**
2 George Cohen	Fulham
3 Bobby Tomson	Wolverhampton W
4 Gordon Milne	Liverpool
5 Maurice Norman	Tottenham Hotspur
6 Bobby Moore	West Ham United
7 Peter Thompson	Liverpool
8 Jimmy Greaves	Tottenham Hotspur
9 Fred Pickering	Everton
10 Terry Venables	Chelsea
11 Alan Hinton	Nottingham Forest
England 2 Belgium 2	

Tangerine Trivia

While the tangerine interest in this fixture lay with Tony Waiters who, to date, is the only Blackpool keeper to play for England in a full international it would be remiss not to mention the England centre forward in this fixture, Fred Pickering. Having arrived on the international scene with a hat trick on his debut against the USA he gained legendary status among the tangerine faithful with a never to be forgotten performance on 13 April 1970.

With the Seasiders needing 2 points from their final 2 games of the season a trip to Deepdale to face our old rivals Preston North End in the first of those games ensured a huge away support. To add spice to the occasion defeat for the home side would guarantee relegation. At the end of a tumultuous ninety minutes, Blackpool had won the game 3 0 and Fred Pickering had scored a hat trick to ensure his name would be remembered in tangerine folklore. After three seasons of second division football, the Seasiders would return to the top flight.

43. England v Wales - 13 November 1964

TONY WAITERS

BRITISH CHAMPIONSHIP

Less than a month after his first Wembley appearance Tony Waiters was back at Wembley to earn his fourth England Cap. Injuries and the continuing search for a potential world cup winning team determined there were five changes from the previous game against Belgium. With only captain Ron Flowers having won more than ten caps the England team was a relatively inexperienced international said.

The Welsh team by comparison contained plenty of international experience and ensured a competitive encounter. With Tony Waiters alive to the Welsh threat and looking to launch the counter attack at every opportunity it was the debutant centre forward, Frank Wignall, who claimed the headlines. A seventeenth minute cross from his Forest team mate Alan Hinton provided the opportunity for a debut goal and a half time lead for the Three Lions.

As the game reached the hour mark another cross from Hinton was met by a thumping header from Wignall to double England's advantage. A seventy-fifth minute goal from the mercurial Welsh left winger Cliff Jones denied Waiters a clean sheet and kept Welsh hopes of a positive result alive. In the event England claimed the win and went on to win a forty-first British Championship.

	18 November 1964 - **England** v Wales	
	Player	Club
1	**Tony Waiters**	**Blackpool**
2	George Cohen	Fulham
3	Bobby Thomson	Wolverhampton W
4	Mike Bailey	Charlton Athletic
5	Ron Flowers	Wolverhampton W
6	Gerry Young	Sheffield Wednesday
7	Peter Thompson	Liverpool
8	Roger Hunt	Liverpool
9	Frank Wignall	Nottingham Forest
10	John Byrne	West Ham United
11	Alan Hinton	Nottingham Forest
	England 2 Wales 1	

What happened next?

Injury and experimentation determined that just three of the starting eleven, Cohen, Flowers and Hunt would make the 1966 World Cup squad while three others, Bailey, Young and Hinton had made their final appearance. Although Tony Waiters retained his place for the next England game, a friendly in the Netherlands, history shows it to be a significant match in terms of consideration for the world cup selection as a further five players made their final appearance for England.

44. England v West Germany
23 February 1966

ALAN BALL

INTERNATIONAL FRIENDLY

When the debate as to who will be selected for the world cup gathers pace there is always a late contender. In 1962 Bobby Moore was selected as an uncapped player and played in all of England's games. in 1966 Alan Ball was a player who made a late run for inclusion in Alf Ramsey's final twenty-two. Having been overlooked by several clubs due to his size he was a sporting advocate of the phrase size doesn't matter!

By the time of his Wembley debut, he had been capped five times and sent off once playing for the under 23 team. Although through much of his career he wore the number 8 shirt his Wembley debut saw him wearing the number 7 shirt, emulating another of the Seasiders greatest players, Stanley Matthews.

Playing in a starting eleven getting ever closer to Ramsey's World Cup-winning team Bally was building an understanding with his midfield partners such as Nobby Stiles and Bobby Charlton. With shirt numbers becoming meaningless Nobby Stiles found himself wearing the number 9 shirt which, in days gone by, would suggest he was centre forward that night. Not a prolific goal scorer, Nobby marked the occasion by scoring his first goal for his country in the forty-first minute to decide the encounter in favour of the Three Lions.

	23 February 1966 - England v West Germany	
	Player	Club
1	Gordon Banks	Leicester City
2	George Cohen	Fulham
3	Keith Newton	Blackburn Rovers
4	Bobby Moore	West Ham United
5	Jack Charlton	Leeds United
6	Norman Hunter	Leeds United
7	**Alan Ball**	**Blackpool**
8	Roger Hunt	Liverpool
9	Nobby Stiles	Manchester United
10	Geoff Hurst	West Ham United
11	Bobby Charlton	Manchester United
	England 1 West Germany 0	

46. England v Yugoslavia 4 May 1966

JIMMY ARMFIELD

INTERNATIONAL FRIENDLY

Eight hundred and ninety-seven days after his forty-first appearance for England Gentlemen Jim was recalled for his forty-second appearance for his country. Injury to the man who replaced him, George Cohen, and club contractual issues leading to the absence of the current England captain Bobby Moore meant that not only did Jim return to the defence, but he also returned to the captaincy.

With the contractual issue placing Moore's World Cup selection in doubt anticipation Ramsey's thinking was to take the tried and tested option. In Jim's autobiography "Right Back to the Beginning" he references the fact that his place in the team and as captain was lost due to injury. With that in mind, he ponders whether had it not been for injury, it might have been Jim that led England to World Cup glory.

Of the eleven starters for this game, only two, Jimmy Greaves and Bobby Charlton had more caps than Jim. In what was described as a powerful performance by England it was first-half goals from those two players that proved decisive against a talented Yugoslavian side. The result meant that Jim's club record sixteenth Wembley appearance had finished like the first, with a win.

	4 May 1966 - **England** v Yugoslavia	
	Player	Club
1	Gordon Banks	Leicester City
2	**Jimmy Armfield**	**Blackpool**
3	Ray Wilson	Everton
4	Martin Peters	West Ham United
5	Jack Charlton	Leeds United
6	Norman Hunter	Leeds United
7	Terry Paine	Southampton
8	Jimmy Greaves	Tottenham Hotspur
9	Bobby Charlton	Manchester United
10	Geoff Hurst	West Ham United
11	Bobby Tambling	Chelsea
	England 2 Yugoslavia 0	

Tangerine Trivia

With the provisional squad of forty players named on April 7, seven had, or would have, links to Blackpool. Everton goalkeeper Gordon West had started his career with Blackpool. Tony Waiters, Jimmy Armfield and Alan Ball were all current players at the time the squad was announced. Gordon Milne and Fred Pickering were yet to wear the tangerine shirt while George Eastham was born in the town in September 1936.

When the squad was reduced to twenty-eight two days after the Yugoslavia game West and Waiters were among the twelve players released. Having made the twenty-eight Fred Pickering subsequently withdrew through injury. On June 18, the final squad of twenty-two was announced with Gordon Milne one of the players released leaving Jimmy Armfield and Alan Ball as the two Blackpool players who would chase the dream of winning the World Cup.

1966 WORLD CUP

FINAL TOURNAMENT

JIMMY ARMFIELD & ALAN BALL

Having returned as captain for the Wembley friendly against former Yugoslavia he retained his place in the team and as captain for the opening game of England's Scandinavian tour against Finland. He was joined in the team by Alan Ball, the last time two Seasiders represented the three lions in the same game.

Unfortunately, Jim picked up an injury that ruled him out of the remainder of the tour and left the right-back position open for George Cohen. Although he retained his place in the squad for the finals history shows he had made his final appearance for England and passed on the mantle of representing Blackpool Football Club to Bally.

THE 1966 WORLD CUP SQUAD

	Player	Club
1	Gordon Banks	Leicester City
2	George Cohen	Fulham
3	Ray Wilson	Everton
4	Nobby Stiles	Manchester United
5	Jack Charlton	Leeds United
6	Bobby Moore	West Ham United
7	**Alan Ball**	**Blackpool**
8	Jimmy Greaves	Tottenham Hotspur
9	Bobby Charlton	Manchester United
10	Geoff Hurst	West Ham United
12	Ron Springett	Sheffield Wednesday
13	Peter Bonetti	Chelsea
14	**Jimmy Armfield**	**Blackpool**
15	Gerry Byrne	Liverpool
16	Martin Peters	West Ham United
17	Ron Flowers	Wolverhampton W
18	Norman Hunter	Leeds United
19	Terry Paine	Southampton
20	Ian Callaghan	Liverpool
21	Roger Hunt	Liverpool
22	George Eastham	Arsenal

Club Representation

The story of the finals is well documented, however a point to make is the club representation within the England squad. The twenty-two players selected were spread between fourteen teams with West Ham, Liverpool and Manchester United each having three squad members. Blackpool and Leeds each had two members with the nine remaining teams having one member each.

By comparison, the twenty-six players selected for the 2022 World Cup finals in Qatar were spread between eleven clubs. Of the eleven clubs five had three or more squad members.

46. England v Uruguay - 11 July 1966

ALAN BALL

UEFA WORLD CUP FINALS MATCH – GROUP 1

In the days leading up to the tournament, Alf Ramsey had stated privately to his players and publicly that he believed England had the players to win the World Cup, Selection for the opening game made Alan Ball the fourth Blackpool player after Matthews (1950 & 54), Mortenson (1950) and Armfield (1962) to play for England in the World Cup Finals. .

With Uruguay setting their stall out to defend Ramsey's contention was difficult to justify as England made an unwanted piece of history by failing to score at Wembley for the first time. The reaction of the Uruguayan players at the final whistle suggested that a draw was their objective as the famous stadium witnessed its first-ever goalless draw in a full international fixture.

11 July 1966 - **England** v Uruguay	
Player	Club
Gordon Banks	Leicester City
George Cohen	Fulham
Ray Wilson	Everton
Nobby Stiles	Manchester United
Jack Charlton	Leeds United
Bobby Moore	West Ham United
Alan Ball	**Blackpool**
Jimmy Greaves	Tottenham Hotspur
Bobby Charlton	Manchester United
Roger Hunt	Liverpool
John Connelly	Manchester United
Englan 0 Uruguay 0	

After the opening game, Bally was left out of the team and Jimmy Armfield was behind George Cohen in the pecking order at right-back. Wins in the remaining two group games against Mexico and France saw England finish top of group one and set up a quarter-final tie with the group 2 runners up, Argentina.

47. England v Argentina - 23 July 1966

ALAN BALL

UEFA WORLD CUP FINALS MATCH – QUARTER-FINAL

In his 1978 autobiography, it's all about a Ball, there is a chapter entitled Rattin. The character in question was Antonio Rattin the Argentinian 1966 World Cup captain. Having been left out, of the group matches against Mexico and France, which England won. There were two changes to the side that had beaten France three days earlier. Injury to Jimmy Greaves saw Geoff Hurst make his world cup finals debut. From a tangerine perspective, Alan Ball returned to the side in place of Ian Callaghan. Although it wasn't known at the time, the World Cup winning eleven was in place.

In Robin Daniels History of Blackpool Football Club, first published in 1972 he has a chapter entitled Mr Perpetual Motion, dedicated to Alan Ball. Disappointed not to have been selected for the previous two games the response from Bally was a performance worthy of his chapter title. Then, as of now, Argentina could delight and disappoint. On this day they chose to disappoint, opting for niggly, spoiling tactics intended to frustrate opponents and spectators alike.

In his autobiography the tangerine firebrand observed the Argentinians had little interest in scoring and were more concerned with spoiling. Rattin was at the heart of this approach and, despite an early caution persisted continued with the fouling and dissent. In the thirty-second minute he received his marching orders. Having been ordered off the Pumas captain took around ten minutes to leave the field.

Despite the man advantage the Argentine approach continued to frustrate England until the seventy-seventh minute when Geoff Hurst headed home a cross from Martin Peters to win the game. Selection for this game meant Alan Ball had become the second Blackpool player, after Jimmy Armfield in 1962, to play in a World Cup quarter-final. Now he would become the first to feature in a World Cup semi-final.

	Player	Club
	23 July 1966 - **England** v Argentina	
1	Gordon Banks	Leicester City
2	George Cohen	Fulham
3	Ray Wilson	Everton
4	Nobby Stiles	Manchester United
5	Jack Charlton	Leeds United
6	Bobby Moore	West Ham United
7	**Alan Ball**	**Blackpool**
21	Roger Hunt	Liverpool
9	Bobby Charlton	Manchester United
10	Geoff Hurst	West Ham United
16	Martin Peters	West Ham United
	England 1 Argentina 0	

Seeing red

Red and yellow cards were introduced for use by referees at the 1970 World Cup finals and the Rattin incident is understood to have been a factor. Rattin contended he didn't know what he was being told when cautioned or sent off due to the language barrier, as the referee was German.

It was also reported the Charlton brothers had been cautioned in the interlude between Rattin being ordered off and actually going off. A top English referee of the period, Ken Aston who had experienced the language excuse, when refereeing in European competitions allegedly had a eureka moment when stopping at a traffic light and thought the amber to red principle could be utilised in football. By brandishing the appropriate cards it would be clear what action was taken by a referee and the system we have today was born!

48. England v Portugal - 26 July 1966

ALAN BALL

UEFA WORLD CUP FINALS MATCH – SEMI-FINAL

Had it not been for a controversial decision by FIFA Alan Ball and his teammates would not have graced Wembley Stadium for the semi-final. The semi-final venues were to be Goodison Park, home of Everton FC, for the England v Portugal tie and Wembley for the encounter between West Germany and the USSR.

A late change in venue approved by the World Cup organising committee saw a full house at Wembley entertained by two talented sides. In his autobiography, Jimmy Armfield reflected that Argentina posed the greatest threat to England progressing to the final. Recognising Portugal were a talented team, in his view, he felt England would prevail if the two sides met.

The game, with Alan Ball at the heart of the England midfield, was considered by many to be the best of the tournament. As Gentleman Jim predicted, England prevailed with the Charlton brothers involved in the key moments. A vintage Bobby Charlton strike from distance put England ahead on the half-hour.

With ten minutes remaining a mix up in the Portuguese defence ended when another unerring strike from Bobby found the back of the net and the door to the World Cup Final was wide open. Two minutes later a goal-bound header was handled on the line by Jack Charlton leading to the concession of a penalty.

In 1966 the punishment was the concession of a penalty kick from which Eusebio, the tournament leading scorer, found the back of the net to add some tension to the remaining minutes. Once the final minutes had been negotiated, England's final place was confirmed, and the players were back in the dressing room Alf Ramsey announced the team would be unchanged for the final.

With that decision made eight different clubs would have provided players for the final game and Blackpool Football Club would be one of them. The question now was could Alan Ball, World Cup finalist, become Alan Ball, World Cup winner?

26 July 1966 - **England** v Portugal	
Player	Club
1 Gordon Banks	Leicester City
2 George Cohen	Fulham
3 Ray Wilson	Everton
4 Nobby Stiles	Manchester United
5 Jack Charlton	Leeds United
6 Bobby Moore	West Ham United
7 **Alan Ball**	**Blackpool**
8 Roger Hunt	Liverpool
9 Bobby Charlton	Manchester United
10 Geoff Hurst	West Ham United
11 Martin Peters	West Ham United
England 2 Portugal 1	

What if?

The stand out question around the Portuguese penalty incident raised is what if today's disciplinary processes had been in place? A red card would for deliberate handball would have followed and England would have been a man down for the final seven minutes. Had they still have gone on to win Jack would have been suspended for the final.

49. England v West Germany - 30 July 1966

ALAN BALL

UEFA WORLD CUP FINAL

"Young man, you will never play a better
game of football than you did today"

Alf Ramsey 30 July 1966

In his autobiography, It's All about a Ball, Alan informs those were Ramsey's words to him after the final. The story of the 1966 World Cup final, a terrific incident packed game, in which Ramsey's pre-tournament prediction, that England will win the World Cup came true, is well documented.

Just as his pre-tournament prediction proved to be true, so was his comment to Alan Ball. He was at the heart of the England performance producing what was surely the best performance of his career on the greatest stage in world football. When interviewed during the BBC Radio 5 World Cup 66 Live fiftieth anniversary broadcast on 30 July 2016 hat trick hero Sir Geoff Hurst remarked that, in his opinion, Alan Ball was the man of the match.

As the world knows West Germany took the lead and England hit back with goals from the West Ham duo of Hurst and Martin Peters. With England on the verge of victory, a goalmouth scramble resulted in a German equaliser. Had Video Assistant Reviews been available in 1966 the equaliser may have been ruled out due to a possible handball and the drama of extra time may not have followed. The basic instruction from Ramsey was to go out and win the trophy again.

In the one-hundredth minute, Bally assisted in possibly the most contentious decision in the history of football. Having powered down the right-wing his cross was superbly controlled by Geoff Hurst who smashed his shot against the underside of the crossbar. Where the ball landed has never been proved and the backspin saw the ball bounce away from the goal. With momentum taking him off the pitch, like the referee, Bally wasn't sure the ball had crossed the line. The referee consulted with his linesman who said the magic word "goal."

England were ahead for the second time and this time the lead was not to be surrendered. With seconds left, and the crowd encroaching onto the pitch believing it was all over, Bobby Moore played a magnificent ball out of defence to put Geoff Hurst on a breakaway,

With Hurst powering up the pitch towards goal Alan Ball was running as hard in the final minute as he had in the first in support, screaming for the pass. The disappointment of not receiving the pass was eased as the German net bulged and the referee's whistle confirmed England as World Cup winners for the first time.

	30 July 1966 - **England** v West Germany	
	Player	Club
1	Gordon Banks	Leicester City
2	George Cohen	Fulham
3	Ray Wilson	Everton
4	Nobby Stiles	Manchester United
5	Jack Charlton	Leeds United
6	Bobby Moore	West Ham United
7	**Alan Ball**	**Blackpool**
8	Roger Hunt	Liverpool
9	Bobby Charlton	Manchester United
10	Geoff Hurst	West Ham United
11	Martin Peters	West Ham United
	England 4 West Germany 2	

WORLD CUP WINNER

BLACKPOOL & ENGLAND

ALAN BALL

On 30 July 1966, the final whistle confirmed England as winners of the World Cup. A short while later Alan Ball joined his team-mates in climbing the thirty-nine steps to the Royal Box to receive the Jules Rimet Trophy and their winner's medals. In the days before substitutes were allowed the only medal recipients were the eleven players involved in the final.

Tangerine Trivia

On 17 August 1966 Alan Ball joined Everton for a then record British transfer fee of £110,000 and went on to win a League Championship winners medal in 1970. He subsequently captained England on six occasions and in February 1980 returned to the Seaside as Blackpool's player-manager.

In November 1981 he played in the first round FA Cup tie against Fylde Coast neighbours Fleetwood. During the game, it was alleged that an opposition player, on completing a nutmeg informed Bally he was over the hill. The response was to point out to his opponent was that at least he had been up the hill. As one of only eleven players to represent England in a World Cup final at football there no disputing his response.

WORLD CUP WINNER

BLACKPOOL & ENGLAND

JIMMY ARMFIELD

By the time of the 1970 World Cup in Mexico substitutes had been introduced to international competition and, whether used in a world cup final or not, would receive a medal. For the 1974 World Cup in West Germany FIFA elected to award medals to all squad members and the practice has remained in place ever since.

In his 2004 autobiography Jimmy reiterated the point that, in 1966, the only recipients of winners medals were the eleven involved in the game. When reflecting on the changes that had taken place since he wondered whether squad members would receive the recognition, they deserve for their contribution to the team effort.

In May 2009, close to forty-three years after Bobby Moore had lifted the World Cup and Alan Ball had become the first Blackpool player to receive a winners medal, FIFA announced it would make a further fourteen medals available to each of the winning nations from 1930 to 1970. This meant the eleven players not involved in the 1966 final would be eligible and Gentleman Jimmy Armfield became the second Blackpool player to receive a World Cup winners medal.

The eleven who belatedly received their medals were:

	Player	Club
8	Jimmy Greaves	Tottenham Hotspur
12	Ron Springett	Sheffield Wednesday
13	Peter Bonetti	Chelsea
14	**Jimmy Armfield**	**Blackpool**
15	Gerry Byrne	Liverpool
17	Ron Flowers	Wolverhampton W
18	Norman Hunter	Leeds United
19	Terry Paine	Southampton
20	Ian Callaghan	Liverpool
22	George Eastham	Arsenal

50. England v Wales - 19 May 1971

GLYN JAMES – WALES

BRITISH CHAMPIONSHIP

With Alan Ball moving on to Everton less than three weeks after becoming a World Cup winner and Jimmy Armfield in the twilight of his career it was close to five years before another seasider graced the Wembley stage. Despite the very Welsh sounding name, Glyn's parents lived in the Shropshire town of Oswestry, five miles from the Welsh border. His eligibility for Wales stems from the fact he was born in a nursing home in Llangollen, just over the Welsh border. Having broken into the Blackpool team in 1960 and first selected for Wales in 1962 unfortunately, the consistency of Mike England restricted Glyn to just five appearances until the 1970-71 season when he was called up to the squad for the British Championship.

Having started watching the Pool in the late sixties a personal memory, from the 7 December 1968, is that he was the first player I saw score a goal in a tangerine shirt. At the time of the fixture, Blackpool were mid-table and opponents Middlesbrough top. Trailing 1 0 in the closing stages Glyn scored a late equaliser with a thumping header to earn the Pool a point.

Although Blackpool were relegated from the first division the end of the 1970-71 season Glyn had been as dependable as ever, appearing in thirty-six of forty-two league games and deserved his call up. With the British Championship reformatted into an end of season tournament playing each of the other home nations over a week was an opportunity to improve on his tally of five caps and become the first Blackpool player to play for Wales in a full international at Wembley.

Having won his sixth full international cap in Wales opening game against Scotland, Glyn was selected to make his Wembley debut. Charged with the task of marking England 1966 World Cup hero Geoff Hurst Glyn produced a fine individual performance to nullify England's number 10, and see the Welsh go away from Wembley with a hard-earned point from a goalless draw.

	Player	Club
	19 May 1971 - England v **Wales**	
1	Gary Sprake	Leeds United
2	Peter Rodrigues	Sheffield Wednesday
3	Rod Thomas	Swindon Town
4	**Glyn James**	**Blackpool**
5	John Roberts	Arsenal
6	Terry Yorath	Leeds United
7	Leighton Phillips	Cardiff City
8	Alan Durban	Derby County
9	Ron Davies	Southampton
10	John Toshack	Liverpool
11	Gil Reece	Sheffield United
12	*Ron Rees*	*Nottingham Forest*
	England 0 Wales 0	
S1	12 - Rees replaced 11 - Reece	

51. England v Scotland – 22 May 1971

TONY GREEN – SCOTLAND

BRITISH CHAMPIONSHIP

Just three days after Glyn James Wembley debut another of Blackpool's 1970-71 relegated squad, Tony Green, made his first and only appearance on the great stage. Signed by former Blackpool and England legend Stan Mortensen from Albion Rovers in May 1967 he soon became a fans favourite and was seen by many as a replacement for Alan Ball.

With a bright future and international football on the horizon, a serious injury at the start of the 1969-70 season caused him to miss Blackpool's entire promotion season. His return came as a substitute against league champions Everton on 19 September 1970. The dual attraction of the return of to action of Tony Green and the return of Alan Ball contributed to a crowd of over 30,000 at Bloomfield Road. A return to his pre-injury form was highlighted with an outstanding performance against West Ham in an FA Cup third-round tie when England captain Bobby Moore was given the run-around by Green who scored twice and provided a typically unselfish assist in a 4 0 win.

His Scotland debut was followed by selection for the British Championships. A first international start against Northern Ireland brought a Wembley debut into focus and the opportunity to renew acquaintance with Bobby Moore. A frenetic start to the game saw both sides score inside five minutes as Martin Peters gave England the lead only to see an Alan Ball own goal send the Tartan Army wild.

With Alan Ball driving England forward and Tony Green doing the same for Scotland, there was immense pride within this fourteen-year-old Blackpool supporter whose ideal outcome was to see them both do well and for England to win. With the first two elements of the wish satisfied the third was delivered courtesy of the Tottenham centre forward Martin Chivers whose goals in the thirtieth and fortieth minutes gave England a 3 1 lead they would not relinquish and secured a forty sixth British Championship.

	22 May 1971 - England v **Scotland**	
	Player	Club
1	Bobby Clark	Aberdeen
2	John Grieg	Rangers
3	Jimmy Brogan	Celtic
4	Billy Bremner	Leeds United
5	Frank McClintock	Arsenal
6	BobbMoncur	Newcastle United
7	Jimmy Johnstone	Celtic
8	Davie Robb	Aberdeen
9	Hugh Curran	Wolverhampton W
10	**Tony Green**	**Blackpool**
11	Peter Cormack	Nottingham Forest
15	*Francis Munro*	*Wolverhampton W*
17	*Drew Jarvie*	*Aidrieonians*
	England 3 Scotland 1	
S1	15 - Munro replaced 9 - Curran 46 m	
S2	17 - Jarvie replaced 10 - **Green** - 82 m	

Tangerine Trivia

Replacement by Aidrieonians Drew Jarvie in the eighty second minute of this pulsating game meant Tony Green became the first Blackpool player to be substituted at Wembley. His appearance was the last of twenty-three Wembley appearances by Blackpool players in the British Championship. Those appearances had been registered by eleven different players of which six were English, four were Scottish and one was Welsh.

Anglo-Italian Summer and a career ended too soon

Anyone unaware of the talents of Tony Green before this game certainly was now. Following on from his excellent performance at Wembley he helped the Pool ease the pain of relegation by winning the Anglo-Italian Cup. An excellent start to the following season saw him return to the first division by virtue of a club record transfer to Newcastle United. Sadly, having won the hearts of the Geordie faithful another serious injury ended his career at the age of twenty-five.

52. England v Northern Ireland
7 February 1979

DEREK SPENCE – NORTHERN IRELAND

EUROPA 80 QUALIFICATION MATCH UEFA GROUP 1

On Wednesday, 13 October 1976 Derek Spence was a third division footballer with Bury and had yet to score an international goal. That night his first international goal arrived and on Saturday 16 October he made his second division debut for Blackpool in a 1 0 win over Nottingham Forest.

Unfortunately, injury restricted the number of appearances he made at Blackpool and a move to Greece to play for Olympiakos followed. Realising he was away from the eyes of the international selectors he sought a return to England which brought him back to the seaside.

His form and goals for Blackpool brought him back into the selector's view and he was included in the squad for a top of the qualifying table clash with England at Wembley. Both nations had beaten Denmark by the odd goal and drawn with the Republic of Ireland. With Northern Ireland having also beaten Bulgaria they had 5 points from 3 games while England had 3 points from 2 games.

Introduced as a fifty-second minute substitute in place of Derby County striker Billy Caskey Derek became the first Blackpool player to be introduced to the Wembley stage as a substitute in a full international and the first to do so for Northern Ireland. With the Irish trailing 3 0 there was little Derek could do to affect the result. A fourth goal ten minutes after his introduction completed the scoring and took England to the top of the group on goal difference.

	Player	Club
	7 February 1979 - England v **Northern Ireland**	
1	Pat Jennings	Arsenal
2	Pat Rice	Arsenal
3	Sammy Nelson	Arsenal
4	Jimmy Nicholl	Manchester United
5	Chris Nicholl	Southampton
6	David McCreery	Manchester United
7	Martin O'Neill	Nottingham Forest
8	Sammy McCilroy	Manchester United
9	Gerry Armstrong	Tottenham Hotspur
10	Billy Caskey	Derby County
11	Terry Cochrane	Middlesbrough
16	*Derek Spence*	*Blackpool*
17	*Chris McGrath*	*Manchester United*
	England 4 Northern Ireland 0	
S1	16 - **Spence** replaced 10 - Caskey 52m	
S2	17 - McGrath replaced 11 - Cochrane 82m	

WEMBLEY OPENS ITS DOORS (WIDER)

After reaching the 1953 FA Cup final it was close to forty years before Blackpool Football Club threatened another Wembley appearance. In the 1961-62 season, they reached the semi-final of the Football League Cup. A Wembley appearance was still 5 years away for finalist in that competition as the finals were two-legged. As the Pool reached the quarter-finals of the competition in the 1966-67, 1968-69, and 1971-72 seasons thoughts of another appearance at the famous stadium might have enter supporters thought processes.

In the 1972-3 season a draw in the fifth round at Molineux against Wolverhampton Wanderers put the Pool into the semi-final draw for the second time. Unfortunately, with a two-legged semi-final against Tottenham awaiting the winners of the replay, Blackpool were beaten 1 0 and the wait would continue.

With the club in decline on and off the pitch two relegations and the need to apply for re-election followed. The prospect through the divisions of a fourth Wembley appearance was a long way away. For the 1983-4 season the Football League introduced the Associate Member Cup for clubs in the lowest two divisions. From the 1984-5 season, the final was hosted at Wembley. Bizarrely, failure had provided a new route to Wembley that, in 1989, the Seasiders nearly completed.

Near miss number 1

Before the 1988-9 season Blackpool had managed just one win in the various incarnations of the trophy and had never gone beyond the preliminary round. Wins away at Wigan and home to Rochdale in the preliminary group stage saw the Pool into round one for the first time. A dramatic recovery from 3 1 down with less than 10 minutes to go against Rotherham followed by a second-round win at Halifax Town brought the twin towers onto the horizon for the first time since that league cup tie 1973.

A packed Bloomfield Road witnessed a quarter-final with Scarborough that was dramatically decided in the closing seconds of extra time. A rash challenge on Andy Garner saw the referee award a penalty kick. Russell Coughlin converted to take the Seasiders into a two-legged semi-final with Bolton Wanderers.

Semi-final – first leg

Memories of the semi-final serve as a reminder of the journeys both clubs had been on since their epic encounter in 1953. Both clubs had spent time in rising and falling through the divisions and experienced turbulence off the pitch. The first leg of the semi-final was played on a rain-sodden night at the dilapidated old Burnden Park ground. With away supporters on the open end of the ground with no escape from the weather, a soaking was guaranteed, and the omens were not good.

In a competitive match of few chances, a volley destined for the top left-hand corner of the goal was surely going to put Blackpool ahead until it was brilliantly saved, by a Wanderers defender! In the days before red cards for such offences, the only decision was to award a penalty kick. Unfortunately, Russell Coughlin, whose precision penalty against Scarborough brought the Pool to this point fired the penalty high over the crossbar.

The feeling that it was not going to be the Seasiders night was confirmed with a late goal for Bolton adding insult to injury. The emotions after a thorough soaking were divided between injustice and optimism. By the time of the return leg, the latter emotion was dominant as the Pool looked to overturn the one-goal deficit in front of another packed house.

Semi-final second leg

At the end of a tense ninety minutes, the home side had levelled the aggregate score at 1 1. As in the first leg, a penalty was to prove crucial to the outcome when Andy Garner was penalised for what would nowadays politely be described as a "soft" handball decision. In protesting his innocence, it was clear to spectators close to the incident the sense of injustice Garner felt at the decision had turned to rage and he was sent off. The penalty was converted and gave Wanderers an aggregate lead they would not relinquish.

In my twenty-one years of watching the Pool, this was the closest the club had got to a return to the twin towers. With Bolton going on to beat Torquay United 4 1 in the final the realisation that Blackpool could have gone to Wembley and possibly won the competition hit home. The question though was, would we get that close again?

Near Miss number 1 1988-89 Sherpa Van Trophy						
R	V	Opponent	Res	F	A	Div
NG3	A	Wigan Athletic	W	2	1	3
NG3	H	Rochdale	W	2	0	4
1	H	Rotherham United	W	4	3	4
2	A	Halifax Town	A	2	0	4
QF	H	Scarborough	W	1	0	4
SF1	A	Bolton Wanderers	L	0	1	3
SF2	H	Bolton Wanderers	D	1	1	Agg 1-2
F	N	Bolton Wanderers 4 Torquay United 1				

Sherpa Vans Trophy Northern Group 3 - Final Table									
Pos	Team	P	W	D	L	F	A	Pts	GD
1	**Blackpool**	**2**	**2**	**0**	**0**	**4**	**1**	**6**	**3**
2	Wigan Athletic	2	1	0	1	2	3	3	-1
3	Rochdale	2	0	0	2	0	4		-4

The 48 teams competing in the Sherpa Vans Trophy were drawn into 16 groups of three. The 16 group winners were guaranteed a home tie against one of the 16 group runners up. Blackpool as winners of northern group 3 were drawn at home in the first round to Rotherham United, who were runners-up in northern group 4.

53. Division 4 play-off final – 31 May 1991

BLACKPOOL v TORQUAY UNITED

1990-91 Season

Just over two years on from the disappointment of not reaching Wembley via the Sherpa Vans Trophy the question of whether the Pool would get to Wembley answered in the affirmative. Following the semi-final defeat, the Pool had avoided relegation only to go down the following season. A change of management brought Graham Carr to the seaside as manager with Billy Ayre as his assistant.

A poor start saw the Seasiders win just one of their first eight games and with the side in the lower reaches of the table, a sense of unease was developing around Bloomfield Road. Although results improved the management combination did not seem to work and on 30 November Graham Carr left the club.

On 1 December Billy Ayre took charge and reaped the benefits of the former managers shrewd piece of work in signing former Pool striker Dave Bamber on loan. A goal in his first game back set the tone as 17 goals in 23 appearances helped the Pool moved into contention for promotion and went into their final game of the season at Walsall knowing a win would secure automatic promotion.

An abiding personal memory of that game was the sight of Colin "Scully" Methven, who became something of a cult hero during his time at Blackpool, down on his haunches when the second Walsall goal went in. Considering his team were winning, it was evidence of how much the Seasiders meant to him!

Restructuring of the league resulted in the Conference League, Champions, Barnet being promoted with no clubs being relegated. This meant the top four teams gained automatic promotion from division four with the clubs positioned from fifth to eighth taking part in the playoffs. A win in this final league fixture would have seen Blackpool placed third, just 1 point behind the champions, demonstrating how small the margins between promotion and a playoff.

Fourth division promotion and play-off places 1990-91									
Pos	Team	P	W	D	L	F	A	Pts	GD
1	Darlington	46	22	17	7	68	38	83	30
2	Stockport County	46	23	13	10	84	47	82	37
3	Hartlepool United	46	24	10	12	67	48	82	19
4	Peterborough United	46	21	17	8	67	45	80	22
5	**Blackpool**	**46**	**23**	**10**	**13**	**78**	**47**	**79**	**31**
6	Burnley	46	23	10	13	70	51	79	19
7	Torquay United	46	18	18	10	64	47	72	17
8	Scunthorpe United	46	20	11	15	71	62	71	9

Semi-final

Disappointing though defeat at Walsall was it was fair to say it presented an interesting alternative, a visit to Wembley for the first time since 1953. To reach the twin towers a two-legged semi-final against Scunthorpe United had to be negotiated. A first-half goal from Tony Rodwell was matched by one from the home side in the second half and the teams came back to Bloomfield Road with the tie all square.

In this game, it was Scunthorpe who struck first and reached halftime with the twin towers in their sights. Inspired by the managers' team talk and roared on by the tangerine faithful ten minutes into the second-half David Eyres netted the equaliser. One felt the Pool were in the ascendancy and ten minutes later Eyres scored again to give the Seasiders a lead they would not relinquish.

Preparing for the return

With Blackpool reaching Wembley a childhood dream had come true, I was going to Wembley to watch my team. Having been to Wembley for international matches I was aware of what the atmosphere could be like, but this would be different as Billy Ayres team were set to follow in the footsteps of Matthews. Mortensen, Armfield, Ball and company by gracing the Wembley turf.

Before that would happen, there was the challenge of getting tickets and arranging transport. Unlike today, tickets had to be purchased from the tiny ticket office located at Bloomfield Road end of the ground. Arriving at the time the ticket office was due to open the queue was already down back Henry Street and curling round the Kop end of the ground. While it was no surprise progress was slow it did come as a surprise when it was announced the ticket office would close for lunch!

Having been in the queue for close to four hours the announcement did not go down well. Fortunately, common sense prevailed, the ticket office didn't close, and the purchase of tickets was completed a short while later. The question of transport was resolved by a work colleague who had booked a coach to depart from the Boars Head public house.

1991 Playoff final

On 31 May 1991, thirteen thousand nine hundred and nine days after Harry Johnston had lifted the FA Cup the tangerine and white of Blackpool Football Club was back at the twin towers. An eight o'clock kick-off meant a lunchtime departure and plenty of time to debate what might happen.

For many, it was the first visit to Wembley which, back in 1991 was a hugely different place to the one we have today. For me, the walk-up Olympic Way is part of the experience and something I look to do on every visit. With previous visits to Wembley being to watch England internationals played in front of crowds of 70000 or more, this visit would be different. With neither Blackpool nor Torquay having a big following a crowd of around 21000 had gathered.

For Torquay, it was their second Wembley visit. Having lost to Bolton in the 1989 Sherpa Van Trophy final many of their supporters had experienced the novelty of that first visit and the disappointment of defeat. As the teams appeared so did the tears which would no doubt reappear at some point during the evening.

For the tangerine faithful the Seasiders made an excellent start with a seventh-minute goal from Paul Groves. Twenty minutes later Torquay equalised, and it truly was game on. As in the semi-finals, a debateable penalty decision affected the game when Dave Bamber was penalised for handball. Conversion of the kick saw Torquay go into half-time with a 2 1 lead.

Personal memory of the second half was of the Pool dominating and continually threatening. The pressure was finally rewarded in the seventy-sixth minute when Andy Garners overhead kick struck the crossbar and was turned into the net by an unfortunate Torquay defender.

Unfortunately, try as they might Billy Ayres team could not find a winner and for the first time, Blackpool would go to extra time in a game at Wembley. Another tangerine first was registered With Torquay having survived the second-half onslaught extra time was a more even contest. Twice the Seagulls had efforts blocked on the line while Dave Bamber had the ball in the net only for the linesman's flag to intervene. With neither team able to break the deadlock penalties were required to determine which team would be promoted.

Penalties at Wembley – Chapter 1

The shoot-out got off to the worst possible start as Tony Rodwell had Blackpool's first kick saved. The feeling of sickness eased as Steve McIlhargey saved the first Torquay spot-kick. Mark Taylor, Ian Gore, Paul Groves and Andy Garner all found the net. Each time the Torquay penalty takers found the net and still the teams could not be separated.

With sudden death needed the outcome of the next penalty was, for me, best summed by a taxi driving friend who once had Dave Bamber in his cab as a customer. The conversation turned to football and penalties. Without thinking he asked his customer if he'd ever taken a penalty. No answer was the reply and the conversation ended.

Sadly, from a tangerine perspective, the next Torquay penalty taker found the net and the tears of disappointment began to flow.

Next up was an epic journey that saw us arrive home around six am. On waking later that day the emotion and experience of the occasion began to sink in along with the realisation that, with the opportunities lower division clubs now had to reach Wembley, if the Pool could do it once maybe they could do it again?

1991 Division 4 Play-off	
1	Steve McIlhargey
2	Mike Davies
3	Alan Wright
4	Paul Groves
5	Phil Horner
6	Ian Gore
7	Tony Rodwell
8	Mark Taylor
9	Dave Bamber
10	Andy Garner
11	David Eyres
12	*Trevor Sinclair*
S1	12 - Sinclair for 2 - Davies 103m

The Road to Wembley 1991						
R	V	Opponent	Res	F	A	Notes
SF1	A	Scunthorpe United	D	1	1	Agg 3-2
SF2	H	Scunthorpe United	W	2	1	
F	N	Torquay United	L	2	2	Pens 4-5

Tangerine trivia

When Mike Davies was substituted in the one hundred and third minute, he became the first seasider to be replaced at Wembley in a club fixture. Tony Green had previously become the first seasider to be substituted at Wembley in an international fixture.

His replacement, Trevor Sinclair, became the first seasider to be introduced to a Wembley final as a substitute in a club fixture. Once the use of substitutes had been established as standard practice within the game the first seasider introduced as a Wembley substitute was Derek Spence in an international fixture.

54. Division 4 Playoff Final - 23 MAY 1992

BLACKPOOL v SCUNTHORPE UNITED

1991-92 Season

It is often said you wait for ages for a bus and then two arrive together. Remarkably. Having waited thirty-eight years for a return to Wembley, twelve months later, we were there again. Likewise, it is often said you shouldn't go back to somewhere you've been before. However, the re-signing of centre forward Dave Bamber following his successful loan spell the previous season was evidence that statement doesn't always ring true. As they had done the previous season the goals came regularly. With Bamber, Paul Groves, David Eyres and Tony Rodwell all reaching double-figure goal tally's there was always a clear goal threat from the Seasiders.

As the season reached its climax there was more than one instance of Deja vu. For the second season running Blackpool went into the last game of the season needing a win to be certain of automatic promotion. This time the venue was Sincil Bank home of Lincoln City. Just as it had 12 months previously, a 2 0 defeat saw the Pool miss automatic promotion and facing the prospect of a two-legged semi-final against Barnet. In the event, a draw would have secured promotion on goal difference while a win would have seen the Pool promoted as runners-up.

Just as it was twelve months earlier disappointment among supporters turned to optimism. Knowing several players had suffered the disappointment of defeat against Torquay, they would not want to repeat the experience.

Fourth division promotion and play-off places 1991-92									
Pos	Team	P	W	D	L	F	A	Pts	GD
1	Burnley	42	25	8	9	79	43	83	36
2	Rotherham United	42	22	11	9	70	37	77	33
3	Mansfield Town	42	23	8	11	75	53	77	22
4	**Blackpool**	**42**	**22**	**10**	**10**	**71**	**45**	**76**	**26**
5	Scunthorpe United	42	21	9	12	64	59	72	5
6	Crewe Alexandra	42	20	10	12	66	51	70	15
7	Barnet	42	21	6	15	81	61	69	20

Semi-final

Whereas the Pools first excursion into the playoffs had seen them take on an established football league club in Scunthorpe their second saw them take on a Barnet side looking to achieve the leap from non-league to division 3 in successive seasons.

The first leg at Underhill on 10 May saw the Pool beaten 1 0 and the teams returned to Bloomfield Road with all to play for. With a first-half goal from Paul Groves and a second-half penalty converted by (ooh) Andy Garner, the tangerine and white colours of Blackpool Football Club would return to Wembley Stadium for the fifth time in their history.

Play-off final

Scunthorpe United, semi-final opponents of the Pool twelve months previously were our final opponents this time. Dave Bamber, who suffered the anguish of missing the sudden death penalty a year earlier gave Blackpool a first-half lead which was cancelled out by a terrific strike from Ian Daws early in the second half. With no further goals, the game moved into extra time and the tension was mounting. With the Pool having the better of the game Bamber and Tony Rodwell both went close.

Without knowing it at the time, possibly the most significant move of the game came at halftime in extra time when substitutes Graham Alexander and Jason White were introduced by the Iron. The final fifteen minutes came and went with the full-time whistle. Penalties again, surely lightning wouldn't strike twice.

Penalties at Wembley – chapter 2

With several players having been here before one hoped it would help the nerves of the Seasiders. The first three Scunthorpe penalties found the net only for Mitch Cook, Andy Garner and Paul Groves to level the scores. Fourth up was one of the Scunthorpe substitutes, Graham Alexander to have his kick saved by Steve McIlhargey. David Eyres found the net and the promotion door was open. The second Scunthorpe substitute, Jason White stepped forward and fired his penalty over the bar. Billy Ayres tangerine army were jubilant and at last, the age-old terrace chant of the Pool are going up had come true.

1992 Division 4 Play-off

1	Steve McIlhargey
2	Dave Burgess
3	Mitch Cook
4	Paul Groves
5	Mike Davies
6	Ian Gore
7	Tony Rodwell
8	Phil Horner
9	Dave Bamber
10	Andy Garner
11	David Eyres
12	*Trevor Sinclair*
13	*Jamie Murphy*

S! 13 - Murphy for 5 - Davies 72m
S2 12 - Sinclair for 8 - Horner 90m

The Road to Wembley 1992						
R	V	Opponent	Res	F	A	Notes
SF1	A	Barnet	L	0	1	
SF2	H	Barnet	W	2	0	Agg 2-1
F	N	Scunthorpe United	W	1	1	Pens 4-3

Tangerine Trivia

Having become Blackpool's first Wembley substitute in 1991, Trevor Sinclair became the first seasider to make two substitute appearances under the Twin Towers. Having been replaced by Sinclair in the 91 final the introduction of Jamie Murphy saw Mike Davies became the first Pool player to be replaced at Wembley on two occasions.

The introduction of Jamie Murphy as a substitute meant the youngster had made his Wembley debut before his league debut. His previous first team appearances had come in an FA Cup tie and the play-off semi-finals.

Penalties at Wembley – the agony and the ecstasy

Having been beaten in the first play-off shoot out in 1991 success in this penalty shoot-out meant Blackpool had become the first team to experience the disappointment of losing and the joy of winning on penalties in play-off finals at Wembley. Paul Groves and Andy Garner became the first players to find the net twice in shoot-outs at Wembley.

Although he missed a penalty during the shoot-out Graham Alexander went to become one of the most successful penalty takers of all-time scoring 77 times from the spot during his 1000 game career.

Twenty- nine years later Gareth Southgate introduced Marcus Rashford and Jadon Sancho as extra time substitutes in the delayed Euro 2020 final against Italy at Wembley. Sadly, like Graham Alexander and Jason White, both failed to score and finished on the losing side.

Seaside spot-kicks

The following is record of every penalty scored by Seasiders at Wembley. Eddie Shimwell's successful spot-kick in the 1948 FA Cup Final was the first goal scored for the Pool at the stadium.

	Player	Outcome	F	A
1	Eddie Shimwell	scored	1	0
1991 penalty shoot-out				
2	Tony Rodwell	saved	0	0
3	Mark Taylor	scored	1	1
4	Ian Gore	scored	2	2
5	Paul Groves	scored	3	3
6	Andy Garner	scored	4	4
7	Dave Bamber	missed	4	5
1992 penalty shoot-out				
8	Mitch Cook	scored	1	1
9	Paul Groves	scored	2	2
10	Andy Garner	scored	3	3
11	David Eyres	scored	4	3

CHANGING TIMES

With Wembley now established as the final venue for many more competitions the possibility of players and supporters having the opportunity to play at or attend the famous stadium had increased. For the fourth time in seven years, the possibility of a Wembley appearance loomed large for the Seasiders.

Near miss number 2

Sam Allardyce had taken charge at Bloomfield Road and for a considerable slice of the 1995-96 season, automatic promotion was very much on the cards. Blackpool had replaced Crewe in the top two in February and an unbeaten run of results saw them top of the table at the end of March. With seven games remaining, in second place, five points adrift of the Seasiders, but with three games in hand were Swindon Town.

Significantly, in fifth place, fourteen points adrift of Blackpool with a game in hand were Oxford United. Three places and six points further back in the table were Bradford City. Back-to-back defeats at Chesterfield and Oxford ended the unbeaten run and, on the 20 April 1996, promotion was achieved at Bloomfield Road, but not by Blackpool, as visitors Swindon Town picked up the point, they needed to confirm their automatic promotion.

The Pools poor run of form continued and on the penultimate weekend of the season, the combination of another defeat and a win by Oxford at Crewe saw the Seasiders drop out of the top two. On the final day of the season, an away win for Blackpool, with no win in six games, and a home defeat for Oxford, winners of their previous four games would secure automatic promotion to the second tier.

While Blackpool ended their bad run by winning at York, Oxford maintained their excellent form and claimed the second automatic promotion spot. A pattern that had developed since the introduction of the play-offs is the form team often ended up being promoted. Bradford City had sneaked into sixth place with a strong finish while Blackpool's end of season form did not inspire confidence.

Add to the equation that Bradford had already beaten Blackpool three times in four meetings the Bantams could not be underestimated. Come the first leg of the semi-final the Seasiders produced a fine performance, winning the game 2 0 and surely had one foot in the final? With nothing to lose in the return leg, Bradford stormed out of the blocks and at the end of ninety minutes the aggregate scores were level. Extra time saw Blackpool hit the woodwork and Bradford netting the third goal that completed the comeback and saw them going to Wembley for a final tie with Notts County.

Missing promotion demonstrated the small margins in football as Bradford went on to win the play-off final and, three seasons later, gained promotion to the Premier League. In the 1999-2000 season, Bradford finished seventeenth in Premier League while Blackpool returned to division two.

Second division promotion and play-off places 1995-96									
Pos	Team	P	W	D	L	F	A	Pts	GD
1	Swindon Town	46	25	17	4	71	34	92	37
2	Oxford United	46	24	11	11	76	39	83	35
3	**Blackpool**	**46**	**23**	**13**	**10**	**67**	**40**	**82**	**27**
4	Notts County	46	21	15	10	63	39	78	24
5	Crewe Alexandra	46	22	7	17	77	60	73	17
6	Bradford City	46	22	7	17	71	69	73	2

Near miss number 2 1995-96						
R	V	Opponent	Res	F	A	Notes
SF1	A	Bradford City	W	2	0	
SF2	H	Bradford City	H	0	3	Agg 2-3
F	N	Bradford City 2 Notts County 0				

A NEW MILLENIUM

WHILE WEMBLEY WAS CLOSED 2000-2007

After the missed opportunities of the 1995-6 season, Sam Allardyce was relieved of his duties and the club meandered through the following seasons before relegation to the bottom tier for the third time in the 1999-2000 season.

During this period there had been much debate about the future of Wembley Stadium. The condition of the building and its geographical location was questioned and there was talk of the development of a new national football stadium in the midlands. The development of the Millennium Stadium in Cardiff was a talking point and highlighted the need for change.

After much deliberation, the decision was taken to replace the historic stadium with a new model more suited to the entertainment needs of the twenty-first century. In 2000 the old stadium saw its last cup final and the last international played there saw England beaten by Germany. Thankfully, by this time I had made several visits and had the satisfaction of seeing my team play at the venue that had been graced by tangerine legends such as Matthews, Armfield and Ball.

Late in the relegation season of 1999-2000, Steve McMahon had been appointed manager when the clubs back was firmly placed against the wall and was unable to stop the rot. Given that his chances of avoiding relegation when appointed where slim McMahon had the opportunity to continue and oversaw the most trophy laden period in the clubs history.

2000-2001 season

Having won third tier title with Swindon Town in the 1995-96 season one hoped he was qualified for the challenge. Key signings were Richie Wellens, a product of the Manchester United youth system and Paul Simpson a veteran of several clubs. The hope was that goals would be provided by big John Murphy, the previous seasons leading scorer, and Brett Ormerod whose recovery from a broken leg would prove to be a major boost.

Early season results were mixed, and a fair amount of time was spent looking down the table rather than up. A 7 0 hammering at Barnet and FA Cup elimination by non-league Yeovil Town provided the lowest points while home and away wins in a two legged league cup tie with championship side Stockport County had been a highlight.

Having hit the depths, the recovery came steadily. The pattern emerging was that a defeat would be followed by two or three wins. With 43 league games gone a play-off pace was achievable if the last three games were won. The opposition would be provided by Rochdale and Barnet at Bloomfield Road finishing with a trip to Darlington.

Three goals in each of the three games saw the Pool place seventh in the table. Despite losing twenty games a play-off place had been achieved. The semi-final opposition would be provided by Hartlepool United who, after being in the top three for much of the season had missed out on automatic promotion.

Third division promotion and play-off places 2000-2001									
Pos	Team	P	W	D	L	F	A	Pts	GD
1	Brighton & Hove Albion	46	28	8	10	73	35	92	38
2	Cardiff City	46	23	13	10	95	58	82	37
3	Chesterfield	46	25	14	7	79	42	80	37
4	Hartlepool United	46	21	14	11	71	54	77	17
5	Leyton Orient	46	20	15	11	59	51	75	8
6	Hull City	46	19	17	10	47	39	74	8
7	**Blackpool**	**46**	**22**	**6**	**18**	**74**	**58**	**72**	**16**

Chesterfield were deducted 9 points for financial irregularities

2001 Semi-finals

Going into the playoffs on the back of three straight wins and two twenty goal strikers in the side confidence was high. A day after minor surgery my attendance at the game was in doubt. The decision to ignore the discomfort was justified as an excellent team performance and two goals from Brett Ormerod and gave the Seasiders a deserved first-leg win. Three days later several of the tangerine faithful had a new viewing experience as the game was televised live and shown on a cinema sized screen at Bloomfield Road .

A superb start to the second leg culminated with a twenty-first minute goal from Brett Ormerod to give the Seasiders a three-goal aggregate advantage. Three goals down with forty-five minutes of the tie left Hartlepool had to throw the kitchen sink at Blackpool. They did just that and pulled a goal back in the forty-eighth minute to offer the home crowd a glimmer of hope. Within minutes John Hills restored the three-goal advantage and took the sting out of the home crowd.

Hartlepool were a beaten side and Brett Ormerod's fourth goal of the tie and twenty-fifth of the season in the closing minutes completed an emphatic 5 1 aggregate victory. With Wembley awaiting demolition all major domestic fixtures were to be played at the Millennium Stadium in Cardiff. Rather than making a sixth Wembley appearance, the class of 2001 would be looking to produce a command performance on a new stage in the capital of Wales rather than the capital of England.

Road to the Millennium 2001							
R	V	Opponent	Res	F	A	Notes	
SF1	H	Hartlepool United	W	2	0		
SF2	A	Hartlepool United	A	3	1	Agg 5-1	
F	N	Leyton Orient	W	4	2		

26 May 2001 - Third Division Play-off final

BLACKPOOL v LEYTON ORIENT

Having visited Cardiff for the first time while the 1999 Rugby Union World Cup was in progress, I was aware of the Stadium's central location within the city. The provision of a football special train was a throwback to away days of seasons past. It meant transport was taken care of and a visit to one of the World's newest sporting arenas was in the offing.

With train travel on a Sunday always likely to be tedious this journey was no exception. While some aspired to time in the pub before the game the better tactic when the train arrived less than an hour before kick-off was to get to the ground and take in the atmosphere.

First impression of the stadium was it was more compact than Wembley and likely to generate a good atmosphere. With butterflies in the stomach hopes of a good start were dashed when keeper Phil Barnes trod on the ball from a back pass leaving Nick Tate the simplest of tasks to put Orient 1 0 up with less than a minute on the clock.

What would it be like if we lost this game to a goal like that? Those were the initial thoughts probing the mind before one thought about the other side of the coin as there was plenty of time to recover. With Orient fans jubilant and Blackpool fans stunned the game restarted and developed into an entertaining and nerve wracking spectacle.

Slowly but surely the Seasiders were asserting themselves and with thirty-five minutes on the clock, found an equaliser, During the season, the Pool had signed Danny Shittu, a colossus of a centre half, on loan from Charlton Athletic. Unfortunately, his loan period ended before the date of the playoff final and with big Danny ineligible McMahon recalled Ian Hughes to the starting line-up.

Although not a managers favourite it was Hughes who lit the tangerine fuse when heading home Paul Simpsons corner to level the scores. The following ten minutes the truly played with the emotions of both sets of fans. Within two minutes of the equaliser, Scott Houghton restored Orients lead to douse the tangerine jubilation. Then with the halftime whistle approaching Hughes central defensive partner, Brian Reid, netted a second equaliser for the Pool.

The half time interval provided the opportunity to reflect on a roller coaster of the first half and raised concerns as to the state of how one's nerves might be at the end of the game. From where I was sitting a fifty-eighth minute strike from Orients Jabo Ibhere was surely destined for the net? The shot struck the post and the belief that this was going to be our day went up a notch. In the seventy-seventh minute of a gripping encounter two of the Pools most influential players combined to provide a moment worthy of, as Harry Johnston put it, a command performance.

For the second time in the game a player treading on the ball proved costly. When an Orient player trod on the ball, Richie Wellens pounced and surged forward. With Brett Ormerod tearing forward in support down the right wing fans, including me, were urging Wellens to make the pass. He didn't and out of the corner of my eye, Paul Simpson could be seen chugging up the left wing. Wellens carried the ball on before delivering a perfectly weighted pass into the path of Simpson. An excellent first touch and textbook strike across the keeper into the far corner sent the tangerine side of the stadium into rapture.

Blackpool were ahead for the first time in an absorbing game and the clock said we were a little over ten minutes from promotion. Surely, we weren't going to win the game outright and avoid the drama of penalties? Those final minutes seem like hours until Brett Ormerod netted his twenty-sixth goal of the season. The job was done surely. There was still time for Orient to go close before a raft of substitutions and the final whistle confirmed Blackpool as the first club to have gained promotion at both legendary stadiums.

	2001 Division 3 Play-off	
1	Phil Barnes	
33	Gary Parkinson	
3	John Hills	
14	Richie Wellens	
6	Brian Reid	
5	Ian Hughes	
12	Danny Coid	
8	Phil Clarkson	
9	John Murphy	
10	Brett Ormerod	
11	Paul Simpson	
7	*Mike Milligan*	
17	*Phil Thompson*	
32	*Jamie Milligan*	
S1	7 - M Milligan for 14 - Wellens 88m	
S1	32 - J Milligan for 25 - Simpson 88m	
S2	17 - Thompson for 10 - Ormerod 89m	

Tangerine trivia

In December 2000 Blackpool, thirteenth in league two had lost to the Conference league leaders Yeovil Town in the FA cup. At the time, twelve places separated the clubs within the pyramid. Following Yeovil's poor finish to the season and Blackpool's promotion, they were two divisions apart!

Brett Ormerod's goal in the final was his fifth in the play-offs setting club record for most play-off goals in a season and a career.

THE WELSH INTERLUDE CONTINUES

In May 1991, a 38 year wait for the seasiders to return to Wembley had been ended in disappointment. Just 12 months later we returned to the twin towers to experience the joy of winning. Any disappointment felt in missing out on another Wembley visit in May 2001 had been compensated for by an excellent game and even better outcome in another magnificent stadium.

As a realist personal hopes at the start of the 2001-02 season were for consolidation in the division and progression of the long promised stadium redevelopment. What didn't feature within the thought process was a return trip to the Millennium Stadium. The forerunner of the LDV Vans Trophy had taken the Pool close to a Wembley return in 1988 and was now set to become a welcome milestone in the club's history.

The format had been tinkered with and the competition was now a straight knockout between teams in the North and South regions. The regional finalists would contest a two-legged area final to determine the finalists. Significant changes to this iteration of the Football League Trophy were the inclusion of conference clubs and the adoption of the "golden goal" which was effectively was, in extra time, next goal wins .

The Road to Cardiff 2001-2002

The draw for the first round saw Blackpool at home to Stoke City who ended the season as first division champions. With clubs moving to an era of resting players and making greater use of fringe players both sides made several changes from their regular elevens. With admission prices reduced a decent crowd saw Blackpool go 3 0 up inside the first half-hour. The potters rallied to pull 2 late goals back and the Pool held on for the win. A 4 0 win away to second division promotion candidates Mansfield Town followed by a 3 0 win at Chesterfield saw the Pool into the last eight of the competition.

A quarter-final tie at Oldham Athletic proved to be a humdinger. Having taken the lead, the home side had a player sent off. Blackpool took full advantage to turn a 1 0 deficit into a 3 1 lead. Despite being a man down Oldham pulled a goal back before two late goals from Richard Walker saw him complete a hat trick and seal a 5 2 win.

Semi-finals

With just four teams left, the matchups for the semi-finals saw Blackpool paired with promotion contenders Huddersfield Town in the northern area final while Cambridge United would face Bristol City in the South. With Bristol and Huddersfield amongst the promotion contenders, Blackpool in the bottom half of the table and Cambridge strong candidates to be relegated the bookies didn't have too much trouble deciding who the favourites were to get to the final.

Following the club-record sale of Brett Ormerod to Southampton McMahon had juggled his striking options to keep the goals coming. With John Murphy and Richard Walker strikers of similar type, the free transfer signing off Scott Taylor from Stockport County provided a useful option.

Although Pool were in the bottom half of the table there was never a serious threat of relegation. Consolidation in the third tier was the aim and winning a trophy would be a bonus. The prospect of a return to Cardiff certainly appealed to fans and a third-minute goal from Richie Wellens gave the Pool an ideal start. A goal from LDV goal machine John Murphy on the half-hour doubled the lead and fans were daring to dream of another Millennium Stadium appearance.

On fifty-six minutes the officials received the full force of the fans fury as a throw-in was, to the naked eye, incorrectly given to the visitors. Sure enough, a goal followed to keep the terriers in touch. The response from the Seasiders was superb as attack followed attack with Scott Taylor proving to be a menace. His efforts were rewarded with a goal and Blackpool took a 3 1 lead into the second leg.

Personally, I have to say the second leg provided one of the single most euphoric moments experienced while watching football, and that came while watching the game in the pub! Huddersfield dominated the early stages and had levelled the aggregate score in the thirty-third minute. A key to the game was the battle between the Pools young central defender, Rhys Day who was being given a torrid time by Huddersfield's experienced front-man Clyde Wijnhard. The youngster learnt a hard lesson that day as the experienced Ian Hughes was introduced as a first-half substitute. With Hughes getting to grips with Wijnhard the home side attacking threat had been blunted and the Pool negotiated the remainder of the ninety minutes without conceding and took the tie to extra time.

Golden Goal

During the nineties, the golden goal rule had been introduced to major football tournaments with a simple basis of the first goal scored in extra time wins the game. The UEFA European Championship finals of 1996 and 2000 had golden goals and the rule was in use in the LDV Vans Trophy.

Having been under pressure for ninety minutes Blackpool started extra time well and fans gathered in the Old England public House in Bispham were more optimistic than they had been during normal time. With the first period of extra time ending a left-wing cross wasn't dealt with by a defender and Martin Bullock lashed the loose ball into the roof of the net to ensure plenty of spilt beer and euphoric reaction as fans realised what had happened and began to think about another day out at the Millennium Stadium.

In the period between May 2001 and March 2002 I had visited Cardiff and taken the opportunity to tour the stadium. One of the innovations of this magnificent stadium was its retractable roof Being booked on the five o'clock tour on a Friday evening proved excellent timing as a poor weather forecast for the weekends Rugby Union international meant the roof was being closed while we toured the stadium. With the roof closure taking forty-five minutes the operation was completed just as we ended an interesting tour.

If Blackpool's win over Huddersfield was a surprise Cambridge United's achievement in beating Bristol City was miraculous. With Bristol chasing promotion and Cambridge strong candidates to be relegated United's 1 0 aggregate win was a shock.

LDV Vans Trophy Final – 24 March 2002

BLACKPOOL v CAMBRIDGE UNITED

Once again, a special train was laid on for supporters to travel to the Welsh capital and with tickets obtained, we were off for another grand day out. Without a doubt, the stadium is one of the best in the world but what it doesn't have is that build-up of excitement as you walk up Olympic Way amongst an ever increasing throng of supporters.

Thankfully, the start to the game was not as dramatic as it had been ten months earlier, with the concession of a first-minute goal. This time we had to wait just six minutes before John Murphy's diving header from Lee Collins cross saw the Pool in front. Full of confidence the Seasiders were dominating the game. Chances came and went, and a rare Cambridge attack ended with the concession of a penalty kick.

The Cambridge captain drilled the ball home, and it was all square. Chances continued to come and go, and the halftime whistle saw the teams level. At halftime, most of the chatter was of disbelief that we weren't winning. Surely it would happen in the second half. Pleasingly the pattern of the game remained the same and happen it did.

In the fifty-fourth minute, John Hills left-wing free-kick found the head of centre half Chris Clarke at the far post and the Pool were back in front. On seventy-seven minutes Hills was on hand to finish a flowing move and the Seasiders had one hand on the trophy. Five minutes later Scott Taylor added a fourth and the Seasiders would bring home the silverware.

Road to the Millennium 2002						
R	V	Opponent	Res	F	A	Div
1	H	Stoke City	W	3	2	2
2	A	Mansfield Town	W	4	0	3
3	A	Chesterfield	W	3	0	2
4	A	Oldham Athletic	W	5	2	2
SF!	H	Huddersfield Town	W	3	1	2
SF2	A	Huddersfield Town	L	1	2	Agg 4-3
F	N	Cambridge United	W	4	1	2

Note

With the semi-final aggregate scores level after 90 minutes of the second leg, the tie went to extra time and was decided by a "golden goal"

2002 LDV Vans Trophy Final	
1	Phil Barnes
4	John O'Kane
3	Tommy Jaszczun
14	Lee Collins
26	Ian Marshall
29	Chris Clarke
24	Martin Bullock
7	Richie Wellens
9	John Murphy
10	Scott Taylor
15	John Hills
5	*Ian Hughes*
11	*Paul Simpson*
25	*Richard Walker*

S1	5 - Hughes for 26 - Marshall
S1	11 - Simpson for 7 - Wellens
S2	25 - Walker for 10 - Taylor

Tangerine Trivia

In a time when burnout issue due excess games frequently arise Blackpool completed an entertaining return season in the third tier having amassed 112 goals in 59 league and cup games. Of those goals 23 were scored in 7 LDV Vans ties.

MILLENNIUM HAT TRICK

Having been deprived of Wembley visits in May 2001 and 2002 the theory of things coming in threes happened as the Seasiders earned the right to visit the Millennium Stadium for the third time in four seasons. Had the original redevelopment plan happened this final would have been at the new Wembley. That said, the Pool faithful were content to return to Cardiff hoping to complete a hat trick of wins.

The Road to Cardiff 2003-2004

In 2002 the Pools goal-laden campaign saw them score twenty-three goals in seven games. Two years later they netted ten goals fewer in the competition and, to the delight of the tangerine faithful, achieved the same outcome. A hat-trick from the LDV goal machine John Murphy hat trick saw off Tranmere Rovers in the first round.

In round two Mike Sheron ended a 19 game drought with his first goal in a tangerine shirt to eliminate Doncaster Rovers. A solitary goal from local boy Matthew Blinkhorn saw Blackpool beat Stockport County at Edgely Park and progress to the quarter-finals. Blackpool's reward for progressing to this stage of the competition was a home tie against non-league Halifax Town.

The run-up to this game was one of the most bizarre in the history of the club as manager Steve McMahon resigned his position only to reappear during the Press Conference and request a chat with the chairperson. Understanding is he asked for his job back and was reinstated.

Consequently, pre-match chatter revolved around another strange episode in our illustrious history rather than the match itself. Once it kicked off attention turned to an entertaining game as Halifax sent their supporters into raptures by taking the lead twice. The first equaliser from Mike Sheron and a second from Danny Coid on the stroke of half time typified the ebb and flow of the game.

At halftime it was difficult to pick a winner. The Seasiders finally took the lead early in the second half with a Scott Taylor goal and saw the game out for a relatively comfortable win and progressed to their third Northern Area final.

As it had in 2002 the semi-final stage of the tournament set up a Roses encounter with the Seasiders at home in the first leg. Scott Taylor's twenty-seventh goal of the season gave Blackpool a first-leg lead over Sheffield Wednesday and set up an enthralling second leg in front of a crowd of twenty thousand plus.

First-half goals from Mike Sheron and Keith Southern lay the platform for an excellent win and a third visit to the Millennium Stadium in four years.

LDV Vans Trophy Final – 21 March 2004

BLACKPOOL v SOUTHEND UNITED

The final presented two new match day experiences for me personally. With our local airport at Squires Gate taking more commercial flights a local travel agent had chartered a plane for the occasion. Swapping a four and a half hour train journey for a thirty-minute flight allowed more time to take in the pre-match atmosphere in the city centre. An uncertain weather forecast resulted in the retractable roof being closed and the game was effectively played indoors.

The pre-match concern for Pool fans was the absence of leading scorer Scott Taylor and a surprise on the substitutes bench with the selection of Steve McMahon junior ahead of semi-final goal scorer Keith Southern who was to become a true tangerine legend.

As in 2002, the Pool started as favourites. In that final John Murphy had opened the scoring after six minutes. This time it took Blackpool's number 9 just two minutes to put the Seasiders in front. Southend were rocked back on their heels and the Seasiders dominated the first half. For all their dominance, the Seasiders didn't add to the early goal and lead 1 0 at halftime. One wondered if they would rue the missed opportunities.

A fifty-fifth minute goal from Danny Coid put Blackpool firmly in control and, for the third time, the silverware on offer at the Millennium Stadium returned to the Fylde coast.

Road to the Millennium 2004						
R	V	Opponent	Res	F	A	Div
1	H	Tranmere Rovers	W	3	2	2
2	H	Doncaster Rovers	W	1	0	3
3	A	Stockport County	W	1	0	2
4	H	Halifax Town	W	3	2	NL
SF!	H	Sheffield Wednesday	W	1	0	2
SF2	A	Sheffield Wednesday	W	2	0	Agg 3-0
F	N	Southend United	W	2	0	3

2004 LDV Vans Trophy Final

13	Lee Jones
2	Simon Grayson
3	Tommy Jaszczun
32	Tony Dinning
6	Mike Flynn
23	Steve Elliott
11	Martin Bullock
7	Richie Wellens
9	John Murphy
8	Mike Sheron
12	Danny Coid
14	*Leam Richardson*
18	*Stephen McMahon*
17	*Matty Blinkhorn*
S1	17 - Blinkhorn for 8 - Sheron 74m
S2	18 - McMahon for 7 - Wellens 90m
S2	14 - Richardson for 11 - Bullock 90m

Tangerine Trivia

For the first time in their history the Blackpool had achieved victory in a cup competition with a 100% record. In their 1953 FA Cup run a replay was needed to overcome Southampton in the sixth round. The Anglo-Italian Cup success of 1971 included a group stage defeat at the hands of AS Roma.

In the 2002 LDV Vans success Martin Bullocks golden goal saw the seasiders through the semi-final on the back of a 2-1 second leg defeat to go with our 3-1 first leg success, winning the tie 4-3 on aggregate.

TO THE ARCH (WEMBLEY REBUILT)

When Dietmar Hamann scored the last goal at the Empire Stadium to secure a 1 0 win for Germany in a World Cup qualifying fixture on 7 October 1999 it wasn't expected to be nearly eight years before the new venue opened. Given the Millennium Stadium development in Cardiff started in September 1997 and completed in time for opening in June 1999 the hope was Wembley would be finished in a similar timescale.

Demolition was due to begin in 2000 and building due to be completed in 2003. Legal, financial and planning issues arose, and demolition of the old stadium finally began in September 2002. The Twin Towers were dismantled in December of that year. Construction delays impacted costs and arrangements were made to continue using alternative venues. With Blackpool missing two Wembley appearances in 2001 and 2002 the delays meant missing out again in 2004 and having to be content with a third trip to the Millennium Stadium. Not that many tangerine fans minded as it took us to another of the world's great sporting arenas.

A completion date of 31 March 2006 came and went before the handover of the stadium to the Football Association finally happened in March 2007. Although a date was announced for viewing of the stadium by residents, it was no surprise there was a delay before the event happened.

With the stadium handover complete football began to be played in the stadium with an under 21 international between England and Italy being the first official match involving professional footballers played there on the 24 March 2007. With a stadium safety certificate granted the first cup final to be contested under the arches was the FA Trophy final between a former football league club, Kidderminster Harriers, and a future football league club, Stevenage Borough.

Two weeks later, on 26 May 2007, Bristol Rovers and Shrewsbury Town became the first clubs from the English Football League to compete at the stadium in the league two play-off final. The following day, it was time to turn the Wembley Arch tangerine for the first time.

55. League One Playoff Final - 27 MAY 2007

BLACKPOOL V YEOVIL TOWN

2006-2007 Season

With Steve McMahon's tenure as Blackpool manager ending at the second attempt in 2004 the prospects of further grand days out at the Millennium Stadium never materialised. Early departures from the Football League trophy, a mid-table finish and a relegation battle under the management of Colin Hendry saw Simon Grayson swap his tangerine shirt for the manager's chair. His achievement in stabilising the team in the closing stages of the 2005-6 season to avoid relegation earned him the right to have a crack at the job for the 2006-7 season.

Just as the proposed Wembley handover didn't go according to plan, nor did the start of Blackpool's season. Defeats and no goals in each of the first three league games and just seven points from ten games suggested another struggle with relegation. However, as the pre and early season signings settled the teams form and results improved. The table was climbed, and the play-offs became a topic of conversation amongst the tangerine faithful.

At the end of January, the Pool had eighteen league games left. Taking seventy-five points as an estimate of what was needed to make the playoffs opinion was ten wins were needed to achieve that target. Elimination from the FA Cup was followed by a run that saw the Seasiders take just one point from four games. A trip to fellow play-off contenders Oldham Athletic on a freezing Tuesday night was seen as a must win fixture. The game was won and triggered a six-game unbeaten run that yielded fourteen points.

Five wins from the last eight games would surely secure a play-off place. Defeat at bottom club Rotherham made the target five wins from seven games. Five games later a Keith Southern goal secured a fifth consecutive win away to Cheltenham Town ensuring a sixth-place finish was the worst the Seasiders would achieve. With automatic promotion still a possibility there was every incentive to keep the winning run going.

The sad passing of Blackpool's World Cup winner Alan Ball on 25 April and the visit of league leaders Scunthorpe on 28 April was a coincidence that galvanised the team and the tangerine faithful. A deserved 3 1 win for the Pool meant the Iron had to wait another week for the result that could confirm them as champions. Results elsewhere meant a win in the final league game at Swansea might yet secure automatic promotion.

With Swansea chasing a play-off place an open exciting game developed. With Andy Morrell (4) and Keigan Parker(2) sharing six goals conceding three was not a concern and third place, with a total of eighty-three points, saw the Seasiders into the league one play-offs. The opposition in the play-off semi-final would be provided by Oldham Athletic who amassed the benchmark seventy-five points in finishing sixth.

League One promotion and play-off places 2006-2007									
Pos	Team	P	W	D	L	F	A	Pts	GD
1	Scunthorpe United	46	26	13	7	73	35	91	38
2	Bristol City	46	25	10	11	63	39	85	22
3	**Blackpool**	**46**	**24**	**11**	**11**	**76**	**49**	**83**	**27**
4	Nottingham Forest	46	23	23	10	65	41	82	24
5	Yeovil Town	46	23	10	13	55	39	79	16
6	Oldham Athletic	46	21	12	13	69	47	75	18

Semi-finals

Qualification for the play-offs generated much optimism and interest on two fronts. A remarkable club record-equalling run of seven consecutive wins and the opening of the new Wembley Stadium meant the Seasiders could be one of the first teams to have played at the new venue.

On Sunday 13 May the Seasiders made their second visit of the season to Boundary Park in Oldham. Having registered one of their twelve away wins there during the regular seasons hopes for a repeat were high. After a goalless first half, the Pool broke the deadlock with a fifty second minute goal from right-back Shaun Barker. With a club record, eighth consecutive win in sight the home side brought the travelling Pool fans back to earth with a seventy-fifth minute penalty to level the scores.

While a draw would have been a decent result the Pool caught their second wind and with three minutes left Wes Hoolahan, the architect of some magical moments during the season produced another one to net a winning goal and secure the record-breaking eighth consecutive win.

Consequently, Saturday 19 May was to be a memorable day for football fans with the official opening of the "new" Wembley and the return of the FA Cup final to its home venue. Preceding the FA Cup final, with a noon kick off supporters arriving at Bloomfield Road would be hoping they would be making the trip in eight days' time.

Although the Pool had their noses in front following the first leg memories of the 1996 play-off drama served as a reminder of what could happen. When a twenty-eighth minute strike from Keith Southern found the Oldham net tangerine hopes of making the trip were on the rise. As the game moved into the second half leading scorer Andy Morrell found himself one on one with the Oldham keeper. A deft little dink saw the ball in the Oldham net and Blackpool were closing in on a first visit to the "new" Wembley.

The concession of a late goal caused the nerves to jangle for a few minutes before a terrific strike from Keigan Parker settled the nerves of all bar one Blackpool fan. The individual in question had made a pre-match bet on Blackpool to win 3 1 combined with Keigan Parker scoring the last goal of the game. For him, a nervy few minutes passed before the referee's whistle confirmed his grand day out at the new Wembley was paid for.

Reflections

The opposition for the final would be Yeovil Town who produced a remarkable turn round following a 2 0 first leg home defeat to beat Nottingham Forest. Six seasons on from upsetting the seasiders in the FA Cup as a non-league club they were looking to upset them again and reach the championship for the first time.

As the excitement of a first trip to the new Wembley grew the first challenge was obtaining tickets. With mission accomplished the following day we could look forward to a grand day out with confidence. Opinion was Blackpool had been the best team in league one for the last thirty or so games of the normal season. Had those standards been achieved for the full forty - six game season automatic promotion would have been achieved.

Having reached the final on the back of a club record nine consecutive wins the now was could we make it a perfect ten? As the excitement built over the week there was time to reflect on the events that set the club on the road to this point in their history.

On 9 May 1978, a 1 0 win for Leyton Orient away to Cardiff City completed an unlikely sequence of results that saw Blackpool relegated to the third tier of English football for the very first time. On 27 May 2007, twenty nine years and eighteen days later the club were ninety minutes away from a return.

Play-off final

An early start saw us travel down and park up at Hillingdon tube station in Uxbridge. A twenty five minute tube ride on the metropolitan line took us to Wembley Park Stadium. Having not been to the stadium since the 1992 play-off final against Scunthorpe the excitement was rising as the new stadium came into view.

The view did not disappoint and the descent down the tube station steps to join the growing throng and make the walk up Olympic Way amongst the fans, merchandise sellers and food trucks brought butterflies to the stomach. Photographs were taken, hands were shaken as old faces were spotted before arriving at the statue of one of England's finest defenders and the first Englishman to lift the World Cup, Bobby Moore.

As a Blackpool fan since the late sixties, one could not forget the day Tony Green gave the great man the run-around in an FA Cup tie at Bloomfield Road, scoring twice in a 4 0 win. Reminiscing over, it was time to find our seats. It is only then you start to comprehend the size of the stadium as you wander round in search of your entrance.

With entrance J found in we went. The interior was more spacious than I remembered from the old stadium and the next challenge was to locate block 133 and find our seats on the twelfth row back from pitch side. First impressions of the stadium were good, as for our choice of seat, maybe not so good. Seated behind the goal at the west end of the ground the cross bar was in our direct line of sight. Little did we know the view would enhance our experience of key moments.

As the stadium filled and the pre-match entertainment progressed the churning in the stomach and the desire for the match to start increased. Three o'clock came with the seasiders defending the west end. With much of the half played in the

Yeovil end of the stadium the nerves were tested as the Pool dominated without being able to make a breakthrough.

With the game entering the final minutes of the half the failure to breakthrough was concerning. As the forty second minute was reached the first of two pivotal moments arrived with the award of a free kick just outside the penalty area. As Yeovil's keeper lined up his wall left-back Robbie Williams sized up his options tales of a comparable situation involving the Pools 1953 hat trick hero, Stan Mortensen , came to mind.

In 1953, Morty's eighty fifth minute free kick found the net to set up a well-documented climax. In 2007 Robbie's sweetly struck free kick curled past the crumbling wall of defenders and found the back of the Yeovil net. Blackpool were ahead and the tangerine end of the stadium was in rapture. With only a couple of minutes to half time surely the seasiders would have the lead.

For the first time in the game Yeovil developed an attack of promise and were awarded a free kick outside the Pool penalty area. A well worked free kick curled over the wall and was coming down under the crossbar until Paul Rachubka tipped the ball over. The subsequent corner was defended, and half time arrived with the door to championship ajar and the seasiders forty five minutes away from going through it.

Half time was a buzz with appreciation of how well Blackpool had played and discussion of what lay ahead for the second half and beyond. Would the Wembley arch be lit up with the tangerine of Blackpool or the green of Yeovil? Ten minutes into the second half we were a step close to the answer as a Yeovil attack was broken up and the ball found its way to Keigan Parker. With defenders backing off he carried the ball down the left flank and, with the penalty area approaching, cut inside and unleashed a superb right foot strike.

From our seat behind the goal, we could see the curl of the ball from outside the line of the post into the back of the net. The door to the championship was wide open and the seasiders would walk through it if they could maintain composure for another thirty minutes or so. In the aftermath of the goal Blackpool were on top and threatened to add to their two goals.

As the game moved into the final stages Yeovil were able to get forward and threaten. Good play saw a right wing cross find the head of striker Marcus Stewart and set up a tense finale, or would it? His close range header into ground bounced up and over the cross bar to the relief of the tangerine end of the stadium.

Moments later the referees whistle brought twenty-nine years of hurt to an end. In my first decade supporting my home town club we had spent all our time in the top two divisions. Back then I envisaged that would always be the case. Now, the tangerine rollercoaster had risen to a new point in its history. Would it stay there, or could it go it higher?

The Road to Wembley 2007							
R	V	Opponent	Res	F	A	Notes	
SF1	A	Oldham Athletic	W	2	1		
SF2	H	Oldham Athletic	W	3	1	Agg 5-2	
F	N	Yeovil Town	W	2	0		

2007 League 1 Play-off		
1	Paul Rachubka	
25	Sean Barker	
6	Robbie Williams	
4	Keith Southern	
5	Mike Jackson	
29	Ian Evatt	
8	Adrian Forbes	
26	Claus Jorgenson	
18	Andy Morrell	
7	Keigan Parker	
27	Wes Hoolahan	
10	*Scott Vernon*	
20	*David Fox*	
30	*Smon Gillett*	
S1	20 - Fox for 8 - Forbes 78m	
S2	10- Vernon for 27 - Hoolahan 86m	
S3	30 - Gillett for 7 - Parker 89m	

56. 22 MAY 2010 CHAMPIONSHIP PLAY OFF FINAL

BLACKPOOL v CARDIFF CITY

2009-10 season

In the aftermath of promotion to the championship in 2007 consolidation in the championship was prioritised and achieved comfortably. The following season players came and went and the opportunity to manage his home town club, Leeds United, took Simon Grayson on to pastures new midway through the 2008-9 season. His assistant, Tony Parkes, stepped into the breach for the second half of the season and for a second consecutive season a mid-table finish was achieved.

What may not have been appreciated is that many of the seeds for what followed had been planted during those two seasons. In July 2007 Stephen Crainey and Gary Taylor-Fletcher had moved to the seaside. Twelve months later they were joined by Alex Baptiste, Matt Gilks and David Vaughan. In the wake of Simon Grayson's departure in January 2009 Charlie Adam and D J Campbell had arrived on loan. In addition, returning to the Pool on a free transfer during that transfer window was fan favourite Brett Ormerod.

Despite steadying the ship in the wake of Grayson's departure Tony Parkes services were not retained and into the tangerine hot seat came one of football's great personalities, Ian Holloway. Charlie Adam returned to Bloomfield Road on a permanent transfer and, although we didn't know it, many pieces of the jigsaw were in place.

The season started quietly with four consecutive draws before an emphatic win over premier league side Wigan Athletic in the league cup and a first league win over Coventry City brought the opening month of the season to a satisfactory conclusion. A superb performance and a win over championship favourites Newcastle in September indicated Blackpool were a force in the division and the clubs baseline target of remaining in the championship was clearly achievable.

With the quality of football produced on occasions thoughts of a trip to the promised land of the premier league were beginning to surface. As loan signings become increasingly significant at every level pf the game that source of obtaining players proved invaluable to the seasiders. The return of DJ Campbell and arrival of Stephen Dobbie enhanced Holloways striking options. In 2007, the loan signing of a full back, Robbie Williams, had a major influence on the final push. In 2010, the loan signing of a young full back from Everton, Seamus Coleman, was to have a similar impact.

Although not able not match the relentless consistency of Newcastle and West Bromwich who would claim the automatic promotion places Blackpool had flirted with the play off positions for much of the season. The primary target of fifty points to ensure championship survival was achieved with nine games to go and the shackles were off.

Six wins, a draw and a defeat away to champions elect Newcastle meant a home win in the final game of the championship season, at home to Bristol City, would secure a play-off place. Although a win would bring certainty the actual equation was the seasiders had to match the final day result achieved by Swansea City. When Bristol City took a sixteenth minute lead the home crowd interest in their fixture went up a notch.

While Swansea's game remained goalless, they remained in the ascendency. When Brett Ormerod's fifty fifth minute header found the Bristol net the advantage returned to Blackpool. With the minutes ticking away the tension was growing, and the final whistle confirmed the league campaign had ended with Blackpool on seventy points. A few anxious minutes later Swansea's result was confirmed as a draw and a championship play-off place awaited our mighty Seasiders!

Championship promotion and play-off positions 2009-10									
Pos	Team	P	W	D	L	F	A	Pts	GD
1	Newcastle United	46	30	12	4	90	35	102	55
2	West Bromwich Albion	46	26	13	7	89	48	91	41
3	Nottingham Forest	46	22	13	11	65	40	79	25
4	Cardiff City	46	22	10	14	73	54	76	19
5	Leicester City	46	21	13	12	61	45	76	16
6	Blackpool	46	19	13	14	74	58	70	16

Semi-finals

The final league placings determined the Pool's semi-final opponents would be Nottingham Forest who had visited Bloomfield Road in the closing weeks of the season. With Blackpool having won that game 3 1 to add to a 1 0 win at the city ground earlier in the season there were grounds for optimism among the tangerine faithful.

A crowd of close to 12000 saw the visitors draw first blood with a thirteenth-minute goal from Chris Cohen. A further thirteen minutes into the game Keith Southern, a scorer in the 2007 league one semi-final at Bloomfield Road, equalised from close range. A tense, competitive game was decided in the fifty-seventh minute when a trip on D J Campbell resulted in the award of a penalty. Charlie Adam converted the spot-kick, and the Seasiders went into the second leg at the City Ground with a slender lead.

What was to follow in that second leg was one of the most exciting games in the history of Blackpool Football Club as the momentum in the game swung from one team to the other. As in the first leg Forest drew first blood when Rob Earnshaw gave Forest a seventh minute lead and levelled the aggregate score at 2 2. Unbeaten in twenty home games and having not conceded a goal at the city ground for twelve hours Forest were surely on their way to Wembley.

Although the Pool had gone behind my view was that, with the goal threat we carried, a goal would come at some point. Add in the facts the last team to win at the city ground that season were Blackpool and we had beaten Forest three times the belief was strong. Half time arrived and Forest had now gone seven hundred and sixty five minutes without conceding a goal.

Five minutes into the second half the belief was justified as D J Campbell equalised for the Pool to kick start one of the most dramatic periods, I can ever recall on a football pitch. Sixty six minutes on the clock and Rob Earnshaw's second goal levelled the aggregate scores at 3 3. The decision to replace tangerine legend Brett Ormerod with Stephen Dobbie reaped instant reward as a wicked deflection to a shot on goal saw Blackpool ahead on aggregate again.

With eighteen minutes left, the seasiders were rampant. In the next eight minutes D J Campbell scored twice to complete one of the most memorable hat tricks in tangerine history and a return to Wembley was in sight. An injury time goal for Forest brought focus back to the clock before the referees whistle confirmed another trip to the new Wembley was in the offing.

Reflections

With Forest beaten and their manager Billy Davies thanked for his inspirational comments after the first leg thoughts turned to something I'd only witnessed once before in person in my fifty plus years of supporting the Pool, the chance to see my team promoted to the top tier of English football.

Unfortunately, I'd missed the dream night at Deepdale in April 1970, when a Fred Pickering hat trick saw Blackpool promoted to division one and Preston relegated to division three, However, four years later I was at Roker Park, the former home of Sunderland football club for the final game of the season. The introduction of a third promotion place meant Blackpool went into the game among a group of clubs in with a chance of going up.

The equation was straight forward. A win for Blackpool and we would be promoted. With ten minutes remaining a Micky Burns goal had the Seasiders on the verge. Inspired by an outstanding save to deny Blackpool a second goal and the Roker roar a barnstorming finish to the game saw Sunderland score two late goals and leave the tangerine faithful wondering what if?

Having seen the Pool less than ten minutes away from top division here we were, thirty-six years later, ninety minutes away. Add in the excitement of another trip to Wembley and the thrill of taking my youngest daughter to the stadium for the first time. Without doubt the 22 May had the potential to be, where football is concerned, the greatest day in my time supporting the Pool.

With tickets and transport sorted one could sense the excitement around the town as the day came closer. Play-off final day arrived, and the tangerine invasion of Wembley was under way. On a glorious day weather wise the sight of cars and coaches adorned with tangerine scarves and flags showing their support for the Pool was a remarkable sight. Memories of tales told to me by my Grandad came to mind. Was this what it was like on FA Cup final day all those years ago?

Once our coach had parked up the challenge was to find the beginning of Olympic Way and let my daughter have her first experience of that magical walk up to the stadium. As we found our way round the stadium perimeter it was an opportunity to reflect on how much the surrounding area had changed since my first visit for an England game in 1977. Finding Macdonald's was a bonus and once we'd eaten and marvelled at the efficiency of the staff in dealing with the endless stream of customers it was time to make the short walk up to the stadium.

Kick-off was a couple of hours away and as supporters of both clubs were arriving familiar faces appeared, photographs were taken, and the game discussed. Bobby Moore's statue was reached and the question of whether he was a talented player was posed by my nine year old. When answering inevitably that January day in 1970, when Tony Green gave him the run around, was mentioned.

In the heat of the midday sun, we thought it best to find our way into the stadium to gain some respite from the heat. Within minutes of the turnstiles opening, we were in our seats and able to people watch as the crowd grew from a few hundred to more than eighty thousand by kick off time.

Finally, kick off time arrived, and the game described as the richest in football was under way. Barring our way to the promised land were the Bluebirds of Cardiff City. Finishing the season 6 points better off than the Pool they had overcome Leicester City in the semi-final to earn their place in the Wembley sunshine.

With formalities over the game was under way and with eighth minutes on the clock the bluebirds drew first blood with a well taken goal from Michael Chopra. Not for the first time, the Pool were behind in a Wembley Cup final. Disappointing as conceding a goal was, it served as a prelude to one of the greatest single moments in tangerine history.

As it was in 1953 and again in 2007 a free kick was central to the tangerine plot. A free kick was awarded to the pool around 25 yards and to the right hand side of goal as we saw it. The Pools number 26, Charlie Adam, fancied his chances. As the deliberations between players continued, we reflected that Charlie had fancied his chances with several free kicks during the season with little success.

With the on field debate continuing my wandering mind wondered what the King of Bloomfield Road, the late Alan Suddick, would have done. Being predominantly right footed an attempt on goal would have been unlikely. However, with Charlie having a wand of a left foot a shot at goal was a tempting option. Finally, the referees whistle went, and the seasiders number 26 produced a magical strike to find the back of the Cardiff net and spark the celebration highlighted on the front cover of this book.

Within minutes, the championships leading scorer, Peter Whittingham, had restored the Bluebirds lead. Back came the seasiders to equalise via Gary Taylor-Fletcher. As the game entered the last moments of the first half the question of whether a player should go back to a former club was answered with an emphatic yes by Brett Ormerod.

In his years wearing a tangerine shirt Brett had become a club legend. Having flourished during Steve McMahons time as Blackpool manager he earned the big money transfer he deserved when moving to Southampton, making an FA cup final appearance in 2003. In the twilight of his career, he returned to Bloomfield Road under the management of Tony Parkes.

At the Millennium Stadium in 2001 Brett had sent the tangerine faithful into raptures with the goal that clinched promotion to division one. On this day, he sent them into a state of delirium by putting the Pool ahead for the first time in a championship play-off final. The referees whistle brought the half to a close and the Pool were forty-five minutes from the top flight. We couldn't (go up) could we?

One doubted the second half would be goalless and expected the nerves would be shredded. While the nerves were tested remarkably there were no further goals and forty years after that dream night at Deepdale Blackpool Football Club would return to the top division of English football. Without doubt the players Ian Holloway selected to appear that glorious May Day in one of the world's great footballing theatres had delivered a command performance worthy of the stage.

The Road to Wembley 2010						
R	V	Opponent	Res	F	A	Notes
SF1	H	Nottingham Forest	W	2	1	
SF2	A	Nottingham Forest	W	4	3	Agg 6-4
F	N	Cardiff City	W	3	2	

2010 Championship Play-off	
21	Matt Gilkes
12	Seamus Colemam
3	Stephen Crainey
4	Keith Southern
15	Alex Baptiste
6	Ian Evatt
12	Gary Taylor-Fletcher
26	Charlie Adam
19	D J Campbell
10	Brett Omerod
11	David Vaughan
9	*Ben Burgess*
29	*Barry Bannan*
33	*Stephen Dobbie*

S1	9 - Burgess for 12 - Taylor-Fletcher 53m
S2	33 - Dobbie for 10 - Omerod 60m
S3	29 - Bannan for 11 - Vaughan 90+2m

57. 29 March 2011 – ENGLAND v GHANA

RICHARD KINGSON – GHANA

INTERNATIONAL FRIENDLY

Promotion to the Premier League generated new trivia, facts and firsts as the season progressed. Increased international recognition for seasiders was one of them and in March 2011 Richard Kingson became the first Blackpool player to feature in an international played at Wembley since Derek Spence in February 1979. In doing so he became the first Blackpool player to make an international appearance at the new stadium.

By making 90 international appearances for Ghana Kingson is the most capped player to have played for the seasiders. Having signed for Blackpool in from Wigan Athletic in October 2010 first team appearances were hard to come by until the Pools first choice keeper Matt Gilks was injured. In March he was selected to make his eighty-seventh appearance for his country in their first ever meeting with England.

With Ghana considered to be one of the 2010 World Cups most entertaining teams a crowd more than 80,000 attended what proved to be a competitive friendly. An early save from Jack Wilshere ensured the third Blackpool keeper to play for his country at Wembley in a full international was involved in the action. An excellent save from Ashley Young kept the game goalless before Andy Carroll netted his first goal for the three lions in the closing minutes of the first half.

An outstanding save from Kingson denied England a second goal on the hour and the resilience and endeavour of Ghana was rewarded in injury time when Asamoah Gyan scored his countries first ever goal against England and earn them a draw from a very entertaining game.

29 November 2011 - England v **Ghana**		
	Player	Club
1	**Richard Kingson**	**Blackpool**
17	Addy Lee	FK Crvena Zvezda
3	Asamoah Gyan	Sunderland
4	John Panstil	Fulham
5	John Mensah	Sunderland
6	Anyjthony Annan	FC Gelsenkirchen-Schalke 04
15	Isaac Vorsah	TSG 1899 Hoffenheim
8	Emmanuel Agemang-Badu	Udinese
18	Dominic Adiyiah	FK Partizan
10	Kwadwo Asamoah	Udinese
11	Suley Muntari	Sunderland
2	*Daniel Opare*	*Standard Liege*
9	*Derek Boateng*	*Getafe*
19	*Jonathan Mensah*	*Grenada*
13	*Andrew Ayew*	*Olympique Marseille*
12	*Prince Tagoe*	*FK Partizan*
7	*Samuel Inkoom*	*FC Dnipro Dnippropetrovsk*
	England 1 Ghana 1	
S1	2 - Opare replaced 17 - Addy 46m	
S1	9 - Boateng replaced 6 - Annan 46m	
S1	19 -Mensah replaced 15 - Vorsah 46m	
S2	13 - Ayew replaced 11 - Muntari 58m	
S3	12 - Prince replaced 18 - Adiyiah 69m	
S4	7 - Inkoom replaced 3 - Asamoah 84m	

58. 19 May 2012 – Championship Playoff final

BLACKPOOL v WEST HAM UNITED

After a remarkable 2010-11 season in the Premier League Blackpool had returned to the Championship. From topping the table on day one to a final day defeat at Old Trafford the seasiders amassed thirty nine points from their thirty eight games. In many other seasons their tally would have been enough to earn another season in the top flight.

During the season, the seasiders had entertained and created unforgettable moments for their players and supporters. With reputations enhanced the likes of Adam, Vaughan and Campbell moved on to pastures new while other warriors such as Gilks, Baptiste, Evatt, Taylor-Fletcher and Crainey remained on the tangerine roller coaster.

With Ian Holloway remaining in charge the development of the Pools fluid and entertaining style of play continued. A mix of promising young players, such as Tom Ince, and experienced campaigners, such as Barry Ferguson and Kevin Phillips, arrived while the likes of Matt Phillips, a fringe player from the previous season, came to the fore.

2011-12 season

The quality of football played by the seasiders continued to be high as were the expectations of the tangerine faithful. As the season progressed the belief was growing that if we've done it once we could do it again. Results early season were mixed and typified by two away fixtures played four days apart. On 29 October, I witnessed a dreadful performance at Turf Moor which saw the Pool beaten 3 1 by Burnley. On 2 November, a superb performance saw them win 5 0 at Elland Road.

Clearly if the latter performance could be repeated on a regular basis there was no reason why promotion could not be achieved. The signing of the veteran striker Kevin Phillips was justified by his habit of scoring goals. Matt Phillips and the emerging Tom Ince were providing goals and assists from the flanks and an interlude from Lomano Lua Lua ensured entertaining football was the order of the day in most games.

An indifferent run of results in March 2012 was followed by a five game unbeaten run which took the seasiders to within

three points of securing a play-off spot. With two games remaining and a Lancashire derby against Burnley the hope was
we would avoid the late tension of two years previously. To the
delight of the tangerine faithful the clarets were beaten 4 0 and
a play-off place was assured with a game to spare.

Championship promotion and play-off positions 2011-12									
Pos	Team	P	W	D	L	F	A	Pts	GD
1	Reading	46	27	8	11	69	41	89	28
2	Southampton	46	26	10	10	85	46	88	39
3	West Ham United	46	24	14	8	81	48	86	33
4	Birmingham City	46	20	16	10	78	51	76	27
5	**Blackpool**	**46**	**20**	**15**	**11**	**79**	**59**	**75**	**20**
6	Cardiff City	46	19	18	9	66	53	75	13

Semi-final

Results on the penultimate weekend of the championship season determined Blackpool and Birmingham City would face
each other in the semi-finals. The only issue to be resolved was
who would be the higher placed club, A draw at Millwall on the
final day of the championship saw Blackpool in fifth place and
facing a trip to Birmingham for the second leg. A good first leg
performance deserved more than a one goal advantage and it
was all to play for in the return fixture at St Andrews.

Five days later a crowd of over twenty eight thousand was in
attendance for a terrific encounter between two of the previous
seasons relegated clubs. In 2010 Stephen Dobbie had been
loaned from Swansea City and played a key role in the promotion push. In March 2012 he returned for his second loan spell
at the seaside. Just as he had in the 2010 semi-final second leg,
he netted a crucial goal to put the seasiders in front on the
stroke off halt-time. Three minutes into the second half Matt
Philips found the Birmingham net and the Pool were 3 0 up on
aggregate. Surely, we were on the way to Wembley again.

As the game entered the last half hour Birmingham threw the
kitchen sink at the seasiders and gained reward with goals from
Nikola Zigic and Curtis Davies to level the score on the night. In
an exciting, nerve shredding final seventeen minutes the Pool
held firm to see the game out for a 2-2 draw and win the tie 3-
2 on aggregate.

Final

In my first ten seasons of watching our mighty seasiders the Pool had frequently threatened to get promoted to the top tier of English football, achieving it once, missing out by the smallest of margins on two occasions and finishing in the top six on a further three occasions.

Since then, Blackpool had threatened promotion to the top division just the once. Two years later we were threatening it again. In keeping with the yo-yo pattern of promotion and relegation between the premier league and the championship the three relegated clubs from the 2010-11 season, Blackpool, Birmingham and West Ham United were contesting the play-offs. With Birmingham beaten it was West Ham who stood in the way of Holloways team. Understandably, the Hammers were favourites, finishing with ten points more than the pool and coming out winners in both championship meetings.

For the third time in six years and the fifth time in all I would be watching the Pool at Wembley. Having witnessed triumph more often than despair the hope was the trend would continue. Accompanied by my youngest daughter for her second Wembley trip an early departure from the Red Lion pub in Bispham ensured we were arrived at the famous stadium in plenty of time to get our bearings, visit McDonalds, walk up Wembley Way and reminisce at the Bobby Moore statue about his achievements and wish the result of that January day in 1971 when the hammers were beaten 4 0 at Bloomfield Road could be repeated in May 2012.

As in 2010, an absorbing match developed with little between the teams. In contrast to the goal laden first half of two seasons earlier the ball found the back of the net just once via a composed finish from Carlton Cole to give the hammers the lead at half time.

Within three minutes of the second half Tom Ince added his name to the list of Blackpool players to score at Wembley Stadium and it truly was game on. Chances came and went at both ends and with extra time looming a scramble in the Pools six yard box saw Ricardo Vaz Te net the goal that would take the hammers back to the premier league and leave the seasiders to face another season in the championship.

The final whistle left mixed feelings as there was little between the teams with West Ham manager Sam Allardyce holding the view Blackpool probably deserved to win the game. Sadly, we didn't, and the journey home was much quieter than the early morning journey to the famous stadium.

The Road to Wembley 2012						
R	V	Opponent	Res	F	A	Notes
SF1	H	Birmingham City	W	1	0	
SF2	A	Birmingham City	D	2	2	Agg 3-2
F	N	West Ham United	l	1	2	

2012 Championship Play-off	
	Matt Gilkes
5	Neal Eardley
3	Stephen Crainey
31	Angel Martinez
15	Alex Baptiste
6	Ian Evatt
16	Barry Ferguson
23	Matt Phillips
7	Stephen Dobbie
9	Kevin Phillips
11	Tom Ince
14	*Ludovic Silvestre*
32	*Nouha Dicko*
35	*Roman Bednar*

S1	14 - Silvestre for 9 - K Phillips 71m
S2	32 - Dicko for 7 - Dobbie 90m
S2	35 - Bednar for 31 - Martinez 90m

Tangerine Trivia

Having been a member of the play-off winning teams of 2007 and 2010 Ian Evatt followed in the footsteps of Matthews, Mortensen , Shimwell and Johnston by becoming the fifth seasider to have appeared in three club fixtures at Wembley, as well as becoming the first to make three appearances at the new stadium. In 2023 he would become the first ex-Pool player to manage a cup winning team at Wembley as Bolton Wanderers beat Plymouth Argyle to win the Football League Trophy.

Twelve months on from a second championship play-off appearance as manager Ian Holloway returned to Wembley and saw the Arch lit up by the colours of his new club Crystal Palace. Sharing the experience with him was Kevin Phillips whose extra time penalty kick decided the outcome in favour of Palace.

59. 28 May 2017 – League 2 Playoff Final

BLACKPOOL v EXETER CITY

In the aftermath of the 2012 Championship play-off defeat at the hands of West Ham it was difficult to comprehend what came next. The signs of decline on the field in the 2012-13 season were followed by a relegation struggle in 2013-14. With unrest amongst the fanbase growing back to back relegations followed and Blackpool's fifteen season round trip from the fourth tier to the first and back again was completed with relegation to division 2 confirmed on the last day of the 2015-16 season.

2016-17 Season

With the club experiencing some of its darkest days off the pitch the appointment of Gary Bowyer as manager came as a surprise and offered a ray of light. Not for the first time, the Pool would reap the benefits of a genuine footballing man with a desire to get back into management.

In the opening weeks of the season the downward spiral threatened to continue as results had the Pool in the lower reaches of the league 2 table. A third round FA Cup replay win over championship side Barnsley offered signs of encouragement at the start of the new year. The away fixture against early season pacesetters Carlisle in February backed up those signs with a dominant 4 1 win. A nine game unbeaten run followed and as the business end of the season approached the seasiders had sixty points from forty games.

Personal opinion has always been that if a club has sixty points from forty games promotion is in reach. Six wins would see that total rise to 78 points which is usually more than enough to secure a play-off place. In the 2000-2001 season seventh place in league 2 was achieved with a total of 72 points. Three wins and a draw from the last six games saw the Pools final points total rise to 70 and secure the final play-off position.

League two promotion and play-off places 2016-17									
Pos	Team	P	W	D	L	F	A	Pts	GD
1	Portsmouth	46	26	9	11	79	40	87	39
2	Plymouth Argyle	46	26	9	11	71	46	87	25
3	Doncaster Rovers	46	25	10	11	85	55	85	30
4	Luton Town	46	20	17	9	70	43	77	27
5	Exeter City	46	21	8	17	75	56	71	19
6	Carlisle United	46	18	17	11	69	68	71	1
7	Blackpool	46	18	16	12	69	46	70	23

Semi-final

The opposition for the semi-final would be provided by Luton Town who had finished fourth in the table on seventy seven points. Parallels could be drawn with the 2000-01 season as the Pools opponents on that occasion, Hartlepool United, had finished with seventy seven points and, like Luton, had done the double over the Pool in the regular season.

The semi-final proved to be a see-saw encounter as the lead swapped hands several times over the two legs with ex Luton striker Mark Cullen proving to be a thorn in the side of his former club. With nineteen minutes gone Cullen gave Blackpool the lead only to see Luton come back strongly and go in at half-time 2 1 up. A terrific strike from Cullen levelled the scores early in the second half before Luton paid the penalty for wrestling with their opponents in dead ball situations. Confident Cullen stepped up to put the seasiders in front for the second time and take a 3 2 lead to Kenilworth Road.

The drama of the first leg was replicated second leg and Cullen was heavily involved again as his right wing cross was converted by Nathan Delfounseo to put the Pool 2 goals in front on aggregate. Heavy pressure from the home side in the closing stages of the first half was rewarded with two goals to tie the scores once again. Half time arrived with aggregate score 4 4 and it was anyone's game.

As the game approached the hour mark a penalty award gave Luton the chance to go ahead in the tie. The chance was taken, and the home side were thirty minutes away from a trip to the new Wembley. With the game moving into its final phase Blackpool needed to chase the game while Luton sought to go for the throat.

With less than a quarter of an hour remaining Cullen broke down the right wing and fired an early cross the keeper had to come for to deny Armand Gnanduillet the chance to score. The cross was met by the strikers head and the ball found the net. All square for the fourth time in the tie the goal took the wind out of the hatters sails and the Pool regained a foothold in the game.

Ninety minutes passed and as the clock moved into the last minute of injury time with the aggregate score tied at 5-5 a Blackpool corner was headed goalward by Kelvin Mellor. The defenders goal line clearance cannoned of his prostrate keeper and into the net. The Luton players sank to the floor. The referees whistle signalled the end of the game. Blackpool were going to Wembley (again).

Final

The 2016-17 season had started for the seasiders with a 2 0 home win over Exeter City. By coincidence, the Grecians had won their playoff semi-final 6 5 on aggregate against early season pacesetters Carlisle United and the two sides would meet again in the final. A goalless game was unlikely and with one hundred and thirty seconds on the clock Mark Cullen claimed his third assist of the playoffs when laying the ball back for Brad Potts to drill the ball home from the edge of the penalty area.

As often happens, an early goal provides the template for an entertaining game with Exeter dominating early possession and Blackpool remaining compact and disciplined. The Grecians gained their reward in the fortieth minute when David Wheeler latched onto a long ball forward and lobbed the advancing Pool keeper Sam Slocomb to send the teams in level at half time.

There was a need for Blackpool to reassert themselves and in the initial stages of the second half they did that culminating with a sixty fourth minute goal to retake the lead. It was role reversal as goal scorer Brad Potts surged down the right. The defenders attempt to block the cross diverted the ball into the path of Mark Cullen who steered it into the net for his fourth goal of the play-offs to add to his three assists.

The entertainment value of the game remained high as Blackpool threatened to finish the job before Exeter came back for the last throw of the promotion dice. In the closing stages Blackpool regained composure and managed the game to its conclusion and, as they had back in the 2000-01 season, turned the spectre of non-league football into promotion.

The Road to Wembley 2017						
R	V	Opponent	Res	F	A	Notes
SF1	H	Luton town	W	3	2	
SF2	A	Luton town	A	3	3	Agg 6-5
F	N	Exeter City	W	2	1	

2017 League 2 Play-off	
1	Sam Slocombe
2	Kelvin Mellor
6	Will Aimson
15	Tom Aldred
5	Clark Robertson
23	Colin Daniel
8	Brad Potts
35	Neil Danns
28	Jack Payne
7	Kyle Vassell
9	Mark Cullen
12	*Jordan Flores*
21	*Bright Osayi-Damuel*
37	*Ian Black*

S1	21 -Osayi-Samuel for 15 - Aldred 31
S2	37 - Black for 28 - Payne 62m
S3	12 - Flores for 9 - Cullen 75m

Three Lions Trivia

Among the opposition players making his Wembley debut in this game was Ollie Watkins. After a second losing appearance on the Wembley stage in 2020 with Brentford in the Championship play-off final he made it third time lucky on the 25 March 2021 with a goalscoring debut for England in a UEFA World Cup qualifying fixture against San Marino

60. 20 MAY 2021 – LEAGUE 1 PLAY OFF FINAL

BLACKPOOL v LINCOLN CITY

*"Late in May 2021, Kenny Dougall he scored 2 not 1,
What a feeling, what a night"*

*Sung to the tune of the Four Seasons Oh What a Night
by the North Stand Choir*

To return to Harry Johnstons introductory quote suggesting a Wembley appearance is like a Command Performance the memories of 20 May 2021 most certainly revolve around Kenny Dougall. Although opportunities to play at Wembley are more common these days there is little doubt some individuals produce moments or a performance that will be remembered forever.

When a player has his name immortalised in song from the terraces there is no doubt what the fans think about the individual. When a player has a dog named after him by the clubs owner, he's clearly made an impression on the man who owns the shop. On 30 May 2021 Kenneth William Dougall from Brisbane, Australia had such an impact and made the perfect start to a memorable week for him personally. Over the course of the next seven days, he made his international debut for his country closely followed by selection in the starting line-up for the first time.

Four years on from their previous visit to Wembley the wind of change had well and truly blown through Blackpool Football Club. In addition the nation had seriously been affected by Covid 19. Having been in the depths of division two at one point in the 2016-17 season Gary Bowyer followed promotion with a top half finish on their return to league one. Alas the off field issues well documented elsewhere took their toll and he resigned just one game into the 2018-19 season. Bowyers assistant manager Terry McPhillips stepped into the breach and did well enough to get the job permanently and saw the club finish two places higher than the previous season. Of greater significance was the change of ownership and the impact it had on the club going forward.

Pre and early season for the 2019-20 season saw departures, returns and new arrivals to the club. Much travelled striker Gary Madine returned as did 2007 promotion winning manager

Simon Grayson. Three consecutive wins got the season off to a decent start and after ten games sixteen points were in the tangerine bank. After a further ten games the Pools record consisted of eight wins, eight draws and four defeats. Liam Feeney was proving to be league ones assist king with Armand Gnanduillett the leading beneficiary in front of goal.

A run of poor results saw just four points taken from the next nine games and the Pool parted company with Simon Grayson for the second time. His assistant, David Dunn stepped into the breach and saw the Pool record back to back wins before the new manager, Neil Critchley, was unveiled. A draw in the Fylde coast derby and a home defeat Tranmere Rovers introduced Critchley to league one football before strangest periods football has known.

With concern increasing over the impact of Covid 19 the wind of change was blowing much further and wider than Bloomfield Road. The pandemic was causing worldwide concern and life as we knew it was all but stopping slowly.

Legislation meant crowds could not gather and sporting fixtures taking place without spectators. After deliberation and debate between clubs and the English Football League it was agreed the league campaign was ended with play-off and promotion places determined by a points per game average. Once the calculations were done Blackpool were placed in the top half of league one for the third consecutive season.

2020-21 Season

Concerns around the pandemic resulted in major sporting events due to happen in 2020 such as the UEFA European Championships and Olympic Games were suspended and rescheduled for 2021. It was decided the 2020-21 season could proceed without spectators in attendance. However, with statistics indicating the spread was slowing the Government eased restrictions and gave permission for limited numbers of fans to attend test events around the country.

Following an opening day defeat one thousand supporters were able to attend the Pools first home game of the season against a Swindon Town team managed by former seasider Richie Wellens. The 2 0 win proved to be a highlight of early season as results were poor and increasing concerns around Covid brought greater restrictions and a return to spectator free sport. As a result, the matchday experience changed from watching the seasiders from block J in all weathers to watching a frustrating internet stream in the comfort of your own home.

As supporters of all clubs adjusted to the changes on the field of play and in the world in general my thoughts turned to the 2006-7 season when an indifferent start to the season ended with a play-off final win under the arches at Wembley. Lightning wouldn't strike twice, would it?

A slow start saw a return of ten points from the first ten games as players and coaches got used to each other and became aware of their individual roles and responsibilities. There were signs of encouragement, not least from a visit to Plough Lane when a Blackpool team reduced to nine by two red cards had Wimbledon hanging on for the win.

The indifference in results generally was reflected by those in cup competitions. In total, between the Carabao Cup, Papa John's Trophy and the FA Cup, Blackpool played a total of ten games but were only beaten once inside ninety minutes. Five of those games were decided by penalty shoots with three of them ending in defeat and two in victory. That one of those defeats came against championship opposition in Stoke City and a win was achieved over premier league opposition in West Bromwich Albion suggesting the Pool weren't a bad side.

Improvement in results saw the Pool reach the half way point in the season with thirty four points on the board. Elimination from the FA Cup at the hands of premier league opposition in Brighton was followed three days later by a thumping 5 0 win away to Wigan Athletic. As the season progressed to its final third, the seasiders were quietly mounting their challenge.

With six games remaining the points total had doubled to sixty eight and the play-offs were in sight. Back to back defeats at Rochdale and at home to Shrewsbury reduced the margin for error in the closing games. Four wins and four clean sheets was the perfect response and a total of eighty points saw the Pool in third place in league one.

League One promotion and play-off places 2020-21									
Pos	Team	P	W	D	L	F	A	Pts	GD
1	Hull City	46	27	8	11	80	38	89	42
2	Peterborough United	46	26	9	11	83	46	87	37
3	**Blackpool**	**46**	**23**	**11**	**12**	**60**	**37**	**80**	**23**
4	Sunderland	46	20	17	9	70	42	77	28
5	Lincoln City	46	22	11	13	69	50	77	50
6	Oxford United	46	22	8	16	77	56	74	22

Semi-finals

With the third place finisher travelling to the sixth place finisher Blackpool would travel to Oxford for the first leg and would do so in front of fans. With Covid restrictions easing clubs were allowed to have 25% of their stadium capacity in attendance. A first goal of the season from Ollie Turton and two from Everton loanee Ellis Simms saw the seasiders record their biggest ever play-off win and bring a commanding lead back to Bloomfield Road.

With the semi-finals coinciding with the week of a twice deferred holiday in North Wales we watched the first leg in a relatively quiet pub. With the second leg to come on Friday and departure due on Saturday there was a dilemma. Go home early or return to the pub? The immediate decision was to stay the distance and watch the second leg in the pub. By Thursday, a change of heart determined we would be home in time and kick off time arrived with my daughter and myself located in the Armfield stand anticipating the Pool would finish the job they had started so well four days earlier.

Nagging doubts brought to the surface by a seventh minute goal for Oxford were quickly dispelled by goals from Elliot Embleton and Kenny Dougall to see the Pool 5 1 up on aggregate. After a frenetic first fifteen minutes the game settled into an entertaining spectacle. Had it been a league fixture it would have been an edge of the seat affair. With the benefit of a three goal lead it was less so.

With forty five minutes of the tie left Oxford needed four goals to force extra time. A fifty second minute goal was the response they needed. Two minutes later Jerry Yates had surely put the tie to bed with his twentieth goal of the season. As the game progressed to its final third Oxford found another equaliser before the referees whistle confirmed a tenth Wembley appearance for the Seasiders.

Play-off final

On the 5 September 1896 Blackpool FC played their first ever football league fixture against Lincoln City at Sincil Bank. Close to 125 years later the two clubs would meet under the arches of the new Wembley Stadium in a bid to evolve their respective roads to redemption. At the end of the 2010-11 season Lincoln had been relegated from the football league while Blackpool were relegated from the premier league.

Transport arrangements meant another early morning departure from the Red Lion Hotel in Bispham, with arrangements made to stop off for refreshments. Unlike the cavalcade of coaches and cars decorated in tangerine travelling to Wembley on previous occasions Covid 19 ensured there would not be a large crowd at Wembley.

Having arrived at the refreshment venue the plan was to set off to Wembley around an hour before kick-off time. Review of the preferred route via google maps indicated an accident had generated congestion to slow the journey. With the merry band of tangerine faithful rounded up a rather tortuous journey to Wembley began. As the minutes ticked by concern began to grow that we wouldn't be in situ for kick off time.

As Wembley came into view the choice was remain on the coach and risk missing kick off or get off and walk. Opting for the latter and finding our way through the retail outlets around Wembley it brought home how different the surrounding area was compared to my first visit way back in 1977.

After a brisk walk and the comedic efforts of the security staff while waiting for temperature checks and searches we found our seats in a sparsely populated Wembley stadium shortly before kick-off. A crowd just below 10000 was the smallest I'd been part of at the venue. Even so it felt special to be there and reflect on the differences between the Pools seventh visit for a play-off final and the first thirty years earlier.

Within a minute of kick off the mind flashed back twenty years to 2001 when Leyton Orient capitalised on an error to take the lead against the Pool with less than 60 seconds on the clock. On this occasion Lincoln hustled out of the blocks and a right wing cross eluded the Imps striker and keeper Chris Maxwell leaving Ollie Turton to register the quickest own goal in play-off history as his attempted clearance hit the back of the net.

Back in 2001 I remember thinking what if we lose 1 0? Drawing inspiration from that day the first thought was there's plenty of time to come back from this. Clearly the seasiders were rocked by the early setback but as the half evolved, they gained more possession and began to pose a threat to the Lincoln goal. As had happened many times over the season the tenacity of Jerry Yates created an opportunity as he chased down and dispossessed a defender. The loose ball found Kevin Stewart who moved the ball on to Kenny Dougall. A feint to the left and a sweet strike into the bottom left-hand corner of the net had the tangerine faithful in raptures. Half time arrived with the scores all square and a record sixth play-off win still possible.

The possibility of that record sixth win increased less than ten minutes into the second half when Jerry Yates perfectly weighted lay off was met with the sweetest of right foot strikes from Kenny Dougall. The ball hit the back of the net again and Kenny's name would be immortalised in the history of Blackpool Football Club. In the immediate aftermath of the second goal the Pool threaten to overwhelm the Imps. As the time ticked on and substitutions were made, the Pool were concentrating on not making mistakes and Lincoln were throwing everyone forward, there a few flutters.

Finally, the referees whistle went for the last time and this most bizarre of seasons had ended with Blackpool Football Club promoted via the play-offs for a record sixth time. The trophy was lifted, the players acknowledged the fans and the enormity of what had been achieved sank in. Back in 1968 I had attended my first game at Bloomfield Road with the Pool in the second tier of English Football. Fifty four years later the Pool had returned to that level of the game. The Pool were going up!

The Road to Wembley 2021						
R	V	Opponent	Res	F	A	Notes
SF1	A	Oxford United	W	3	0	
SF2	H	Oxford United	D	3	3	Agg 6-3
F	N	Lincoln City	W	2	1	

	2021 League 1 Play-off	
1	Chris Maxwell	
20	Ollie Turton	
29	Luke Garbutt	
39	Kevin Stewart	
26	Dan Ballard	
3	James Husband	
8	Keshi Anderson	
12	Kenny Dougall	
9	Jerry Yates	
32	Elliot Embleton	
15	Demi Mitchell	
18	*Grant Ward*	
4	*Jordan Thornily*	
22	*C J Hamilton*	
14	*Gary Madine*	
S1	14 - Madine for 15 - Mitchell 69m	
S2	18 Ward for 8 - Anderson 79m	
S2	22 Hamilton for 32 - Embleton 79m	
S3	4 Thorniley for 9 - Yates 90m	

Part two – appearances at Wembley

This part of this book will provide reference to each of the one hundred and nine Blackpool players who have made an appearance for club and / or country starting with Jimmy Armfield, who made sixteen appearances counting down to those who played at the old or new stadium just once.

Where two or more players have featured in the same fixture(s) reference will be made under the details of the fixture. For example 5 players made their only Wembley appearance in the 1948 FA Cup Final while 10 players appeared in the play-off finals of 1991 and 1992.

16 Appearances – Jimmy Armfield

App	Jimmy Armfield	Oppnent	Date	Fix	Notes
1	England U23	Rumania U23	16/10/1957	F	W 3-2
2	England	Yugoslavia	11/05/1960	F	D 3-3
3	England	Spain	26/10/1960	BC	W 4-2
4	England	Wales	23/11/1960	BC	W 5-1
5	England	Scotland	15/04/1961	BC	W 9-3
6	England	Mexico	10/05/1961	F	W 8-0
7	England	Portugal	25/10/1961	F	W 2-0
8	England	Northern Ireland	22/11/1961	BC	D 1-1
9	England	Austria	04/04/1962	F	W 3-1
10	England	Switzerland	09/05/1962	F	W 3-1
11	England	Wales	21/11/1962	BC	W 4-0
12	England	Scotland	06/04/1963	BC	L 1-2
13	England	Brazil	08/05/1963	F	D 1-1
14	England	Rest of World	23/10/1963	F	W 2-1
15	England	Northern Ireland	20/11/1963	BC	W 8-3
16	England	Yugoslavia	04/05/1966	F	W 2-0

Status	P	W	D	L	Captain
U23-f	1	1	0	0	
F	8	6	2	0	3
BC	7	5	1	1	3
Total	16	12	3	1	6

Status	P	W	D	L
F	3	1	1	0
BC	3	2	1	1
Total	6	3	2	1

Leading the way with a club record 16 Wembley appearances is Jimm Armfield. In his international career he made a club record 43 appearances for England captaining the team on 15 occasions and leading them out 6 times at Wembley. Prior to his full international debut, he made 6 Appearances for the England under 23 side, 1 of which was played at Wembley, captaining the team on 4 occasions. In 1962 he became the third Blackpool player, after Matthews and Mortensen , to play in the World Cup finals for England and the first from any of the home nations to be involved in a quarter final.

15 Appearances – Sir Stanley Matthews

App	Stan Matthews	Opponent	Date	Fix	Notes
1	Blackpool	Manchester United	24/04/1948	FAC	L 2-4
2	England	Scotland	09/04/1949	BC	L 1-3
3	England	Scotland	14/04/1951	BC	L 2-3
4	Blackpool	Newcastle United	28/04/1951	FAC	L 0-2
5	Blackpool	Bolton Wanderers	02/05/1953	FAC	W 4-3
6	England	Rest of Europe	21/10/1953	F	D 4-4
7	England	Hungary	25/11/1953	F	L 3-6
8	England	Wales	10/11/1954	BC	W 3-2
9	England	West Germany	01/12/1954	F	W 3-1
10	England	Scotland	02/04/1955	BC	W 7-2
11	England	Brazil	09/05/1956	F	W 4-2
12	England	Wales	14/11/1956	BC	W 3-1
13	England	Yugoslavia	28/11/1956	F	W 2-0
14	England	Scotland	06/04/1957	BC	W 2-1
15	England	Republic of Ireland	08/05/1957	WCQ	W 5-1

Wembley Record				
Status	P	W	D	L
FAC	3	1	0	2
F	5	3	1	1
BC	6	4	0	2
WCQ	1	1	0	0
Total	15	9	1	5

By the time Sir Stan made his move from the Potteries to the Seaside he was already a seasoned international. In his time at Blackpool, he won a further 36 England caps to set a club record later broken by Jimmy Armfield. His 3 Wembley appearances for Blackpool were supplemented by a further 12 appearances for England.

In 1956 he became the first ever European Footballer of the year and in 1957 made his final England appearance in the first World Cup qualifying fixture played at Wembley, against Ireland.

10 Appearances – Stan Mortensen

App	Stan Mortenson	Opponent	Date	Fix	Result	Goals
1	Wales	England	25/09/1943	War	L 3-8	
2	Comb Ser	Metropolitan Police	09/05/1945	Ch	W 3-1	2
3	Blackpool	Manchester United	24/04/1948	CF	L 2-4	1
4	England	Scotland	09/04/1949	BC	L 1-3	
5	England	Scotland	14/04/1951	BC	L 2-3	
6	Blackpool	Newcastle United	28/04/1951	CF	L 0-2	
7	England	Argentina	09/05/1951	F	W 2-1	1
8	Blackpool	Bolton Wanderers	02/05/1953	CF	W 4-3	3
9	England	Rest of Europe	21/10/1953	F	D 4-4	1
10	England	Hungary	25/11/1953	F	L 3-6	1

	Wembley Record					For
Status	P	W	D	L	Goals	
FAC	3	1	0	2	4	Blackpool
F	3	1	1	1	3	England
BC	2	0	0	2		England
War	1	0	0	1		Wales
Ch	1	1	0	0	2	Combined Services
Total	10	3	1	6	9	

Third on the Wembley appearance list is one of Blackpool's greatest ever goal scorers, Stan Mortensen . Morty was as prolific at international level as he was at club level scoring 23 goals in 25 appearances.

At the time of his final appearance against Hungary he ranked third behind Steve Bloomer and Vivian Woodward (both 28) in the list of leading scorers for the Three Lions.

Remarkably his 10 Wembley appearances were shared between 4 different teams as war time appearances for Wales and the Combined Services were followed by further visits with Blackpool and England. His return of 9 goals in those 10 appearances make him the Seasiders leading Wembley goal scorer.

6 Appearances – Harry Johnston

App	Harry Johnston	Opponent	Date	Fix	Result
1	England	Scotland	12/04/1947	BC	D 1-1
2	Blackpool	Manchester United	24/04/1948	CF	L 2-4
3	England	Scotland	14/04/1951	BC	L 2-5
4	Blackpool	Newcastle United	28/04/1951	CF	L 0-2
5	Blackpool	Bolton Wanderers	02/05/1953	CF	W 4-3
6	England	Hungary	25/11/1953	F	L 3-6

Wembley Record					
Status	P	W	D	L	Captain
FAC	3	1	0	2	3
BC	2	0	1	1	
F	1	0	0	1	
Total	6	1	1	4	3

In fourth place on the Seasiders Wembley appearance list is the man who was the first to receive the FA Cup from Her Royal Highness Queen Elizabeth II. In his 6 appearances on the Wembley stage, he was only on the winning side once. That said, the one win came in the highest point of the history of Blackpool Football Club and ensured he joined the 2 Stans, Matthews and Mortensen , in the third time lucky club.

Indeed, after his Wembley debut against Scotland in 1947 he shared the stage with the 2 Stans in his 5 remaining appearances as all 3 were selected for the British Championship fixture against Scotland in 1951 and the friendly against Hungary in 1953.

5 Appearances – Alan Ball

App	Alan Ball	Opponent	Date	Fix	Result
1	England	West Germany	23/02/1966	F	W 1-0
2	England	Uruguay	11/07/1966	WCG	D 0-0
3	England	Argentina	23/07/1966	WCQ	W 1-0
4	England	Portugal	26/07/1966	WCS	W 2-1
5	England	West Germany	30/07/1966	WCF	W 4-2

Wembley Record				
Status	P	W	D	L
WC	4	3	1	0
F	1	1	0	0
Total	5	4	1	0

While 3 of the 4 Seasiders in front of Bally were present on the greatest day in the history of Blackpool Football Club it is fair to say he was present on the greatest day in the history of English Football to date. Rejected by clubs due to his size he went on to prove that, if you are good enough, size really doesn't matter.

On the 9 May 1965 he made his England debut. On 26 June 1966 he was selected for his eighth appearance for the Three Lions on the occasion club colleague Jimmy Armfield returned to win his forty second cap. Thirty four days later his tally of international appearance had swelled to fourteen and he was a World Cup winner.

Each game he played in the World Cup finals was provided a historic milestone as opening game against Uruguay was the first goalless draw in an international at Wembley. The win over Argentina was England's first win in a quarter final. The first ever appearances in a semi-final and a final resulted in England's first and, to date, only wins at that stage of the tournament.

Within days of becoming a World Cup winner "Bally" had swapped the tangerine of Blackpool for the blue of Everton for a British record transfer fee of £112,000. For all his success for club and country without doubt, his greatest day came while an employee of Blackpool Football Club.

4 Appearances – Bill Perry

App	Bill Perry	Opponent	Date	Fix	
1	Blackpool	Newcastle United	28/04/1951	CF	L 0-2
2	Blackpool	Bolton Wanderers	02/05/1953	CF	W 4-3
3	England	Northern Ireland	02/11/1955	BC	W 3-0
4	England	Spain	30/11/1955	F	W 4-1

	Wembley Record				
Status	P	W	D	L	Goals
FAC	2	1	0	1	1
F	1	1	0	0	2
BC	1	1	0	0	
Total	4	3	0	1	3

With the contributions of the two Stans taking the media headlines in the 1953 FA Cup final the contribution of Bill Perry is often overlooked. The simple fact is his dramatic goal in that final is arguably the most significant in the history of Blackpool Football Club. A powerful left winger with an eye for goal Bill is one of three goal scoring centurions, alongside Morty and Scotland's Jackie Mudie to feature in the seasiders forward line during the 1950's.

His most prolific season was the 1955-56 season in which his 20 league goals helped the Seasiders to their highest ever league finish, second, behind Manchester United. It was during that season the call to international duty came and, with 2 goals in a friendly against Spain, he became the second Blackpool player, after Morty, to score at Wembley for club and country.

On Christmas day in 1958, he gave Blackpool fans a memorable present, scoring a hat trick in a derby day win over Preston North End at Bloomfield Road.

3 Appearances – Eddie Shimwell

App	Eddie Shimwell	Opponent	Date	Fix	Result
1	Blackpool	Manchester United	24/04/1948	CF	L 2-4
2	Blackpool	Newcastle United	28/04/1951	CF	L 0-2
3	Blackpool	Bolton Wanderers	02/05/1953	CF	W 4-3

	Wembley Record					
Status	P	W	D	L	Goals	Note
FAC	3	1	0	2	1	Pen

As one of the ten Blackpool players to have made 3 or more Wembley appearances Eddie Shimwell was the first to do so without making an international appearance at the stadium. In the 1947-48 cup final he scored one of the most significant goals in the history of the competition and the club.

When converting a twelfth minute penalty kick to put Blackpool ahead against Manchester United Eddie became the first "full back" to score in a Wembley FA Cup final. The goal also made him the first Blackpool player to score for the club at the famous stadium. To date, he is the only Blackpool player to have scored at Wembley from the penalty spot (excluding penalty shoot-outs).

3 Appearances – George Farm

App	George Farm	Opponent	date	Fix	Result
1	Blackpool	Newcastle United	28/04/1951	CF	L 0-2
2	Scotland	England	18/04/1953	BC	D 2-2
3	Blackpool	Bolton Wanderers	02/05/1953	CF	W 4-3

Wembley Record				
Status	P	W	D	L
FAC	2	1	0	1
BC	1	0	1	0
Total	3	1	1	1

One of many bargain transfers from north of the border George Farm signed for Blackpool from Hibernian on a free transfer in September 1948. He remained with the seasiders until 1960 when returning to Scotland to join Queen of the South. By the time he returned he had exceeded 450 football league appearance for Blackpool and been capped 10 times by Scotland.

Having made his first Wembley appearance in the 1951 FA Cup final defeat by Newcastle he made 2 further appearances in the space a fortnight in the spring of 1953. Having become the fourth seasider after Johnston, Matthews and Mortensen to play at Wembley for club and country he returned just 2 weeks later to play his part in the 1953 FA Cup final .

On returning to Scotland George went into management and, 15 years after that glorious Wembley day, managed the Dunfermline Athletic team that won the Scottish FA Cup at Hampden Park.

3 Appearances – Jackie Mudie

App	Jackie Mudie	Opponent	Date	Fix	Result
1	Blackpool	Newcastle United	28/04/1951	CF	L 0-2
2	Blackpool	Bolton Wanderers	02/05/1953	CF	W 4-3
3	Scotland	England	06/04/1957	BC	L 1-2

Wembley Record				
Status	P	W	D	L
FAC	2	1	0	1
BC	1	0	0	1
Total	3	1	0	2

Over his time with Blackpool Football Club John Knight (Jackie) Mudie proved to be another jewel signed from North of Hadrian's Wall. Signed as a professional in 1947 he went on to become one of the club's greatest goal scorers and became one of only half a dozen seasiders to play in the final stages of a World Cup.

Having made his first team debut in the 1949-50 season Mudie spent the first half of the decade competing for the inside forward positions with Allan Brown, Stan Mortensen and Ernie Taylor. In the second half of the decade the departure of Morty to Hull City saw a rise in Mudie's seasonal appearance and goal tallies. Indeed the 3 seasons from 1955 to 58 saw Mudie score just over half of his 155 goals for the club and make 17 international appearances for Scotland helping them to qualify for the 1958 World Cup finals.

Like several players Mudie shared the Wembley stage with Stanley Matthews. On the first two occasions, in 1951 and 1953 they shared the pitch in the quest to bring the FA Cup back to Bloomfield Road. On the third occasion, on the 6 April 1957, they were on opposite sides in the England v Scotland fixture, the first time two Blackpool players had been in opposition in a full international.

3 Appearances – Ian Evatt

App	Ian Evatt	Opponent	Date	Fix	Result
1	Blackpool	Yeovil Town	27/05/2007	POF	W 2-0
2	Blackpool	Cardiff City	22/05/2010	POF	W 3-2
3	Blackpool	West Ham United	19/05/2012	POF	L 1-2

Having initially signed on loan from Queens Park Rangers at the beginning of the 2006-7 season the move became permanent in January 2007 when his parent club terminated his contract. He clearly knew he was onto something good as the season ended in glory under the Arch at the new Wembley Stadium as Blackpool beat Yeovil Town 2 0 to end a 29 season wait to return to the second tier of English football.

In his seven seasons at the club "Evo" as he was often called became the cornerstone at the heart of the Blackpool defence. With the departure of Simon Grayson Evo was reunited with the manager who had signed him for Queens Park Rangers, Ian Holloway. Remarkably, at the end of the 2009-10 season he was back at Wembley to help the Seasiders achieve what many thought impossible, gaining promotion to Premier League following a nerve shredding 3 2 win over Cardiff City. Along with Keith Southern, Evo had triumphed under the Arches for the second time.

After a terrific 2010-11 in which seasiders won the seasiders won 10 and drew 9 of their 38 premier league fate determined that, for the second time in my 50 plus seasons of supporting the Pool they were relegated after just one season in the top division. Ian Evatt was, without doubt one of the standout players and formed the backbone of the side that chased a championship playoff place for the second time.

In five years from 1946 to 1953 four legendary seasiders, Shimwell, Johnston, Matthews and Mortensen graced the Wembley turf three times with the Pool. In 2012 Ian Evatt emulated their Wembley treble and became the first seasider to do so at the new Wembley.

Unfortunately, whereas the quartet from Blackpool's golden era made it third time lucky for Evo, it proved to be third time unlucky. In 1953, with extra time looming Bill Perry had netted a dramatic late winner for the Pool. In 2012, with extra time moments away, Ricardo Vaz Te scored to send West Ham

United back to the Premier League and deny Evo a hat trick of Wembley wins.

Wembley Record				
Status	P	W	D	L
POF	3	2	0	1

2 Appearances

"Jock" Dodds

App	Jock Dodds	Opponent	Date	Fix	Result	Goals
1	Scotland	England	10/10/1942	W	D 0-0	
2	Scotland	England	19/02/1944	W	L 2-6	2

Signed by Joe Smith for a fee of £10000 in March 1939 Ephraim "Jock" Dodds proved to be a prolific goal scorer for club and country. Unfortunately, records do not recognise his feats as football was suspended due to the outbreak of war. Playing in the final 12 games of the 1938-39 season Jock scored 10 goals to finish as the clubs joint top scorer alongside Willie Buchan. His goalscoring continued into the following season with 3 goals in 3 games placing Blackpool on top of division 1 when war broke out.

Once war time football got under way Dodds was unstoppable scoring more than 200 goals for the pool. During the war years he was selected for Scotland on 8 occasions with 2 of appearances being made at Wembley. The first of his appearances while with the seasiders saw him become the first Blackpool player to be involved in a goalless draw at the stadium. The two goals he scored on his second appearance, in the 6-2 defeat, were the first scored at the stadium by a Blackpool player.

The return to peace time brought the return of the FA Cup but not league competition. With cup ties played over 2 legs Dodd played in 5 cup ties scoring 5 goals. The resumption of league football in the 1946-7 season saw him move on to Everton.

Wembley Record					
Status	P	W	D	L	Goals
WT	2	0	1	1	2

Eric Hayward & Hughie Kelly

App		Opponent	Date	Fix	Result
1	Blackpool	Manchester United	24/04/1948	CF	L 2-4
2	Blackpool	Newcastle United	28/04/1951	CF	L 0-2

Having been two-thirds of a formidable half back line alongside skipper Harry Johnston in the 1948 and 1951 cup finals both players missed out on the 1953 triumph for different reasons. Haywood had signed for Blackpool before the outbreak of war and continued his career at the seaside once football returned. Having helped the team to two top five finishes as well as the cup finals he retired at the end of the 1951-52 season, a decision that cleared a path for Ewan Fenton to become a first team regular.

By contrast, Hughie Kelly had the misfortune to miss playing in the clubs greatest day through injury. In Blackpool's penultimate league game of the season, he had the misfortune to suffer a broken ankle allowing Cyril Robinson the opportunity to take the stage for the seasiders.

Such was the esteem in which he was held the club directors obtained permission from the Football Association for a special medal to be cast as a substitute for the one they believed he would have won.

Wembley Record				
Status	P	W	D	L
FAC	2	0	0	2

Ernie Taylor

App	Ernie Taylor	Opponent	Date	Fix	Result
1	Blackpool	Bolton Wanderers	02/05/1953	CF	W 4-3
2	England	Hungary	25/11/1953	F	L 3-6

Having made an impression with his performance in Newcastle's 1951 FA Cup final win over Blackpool the court jester, as he was sometimes known, signed for the seasiders on 10 October 1951. Finding his way into a formidable forward he was arguably the unsung hero of the 1953 Cup Final win over Bolton. While Matthews, Mortensen and Perry hit the headlines for their contributions it was a crisp and accurate supply of passes from the jester to the wizard that was the starting point of a dramatic comeback.

Performances earned him an England call up on a historic night for Blackpool FC as one of four seasiders selected for the visit of Hungary. Sadly, with England outclassed and convincingly beaten, it was to be his only full international appearance for the three lions.

His subsequent appearance for Manchester United in the 1958 FA Cup final made him the first player to play for three different teams in an FA Cup final and meant he had performed on the Wembley stage for four different teams.

Wembley Record			
Status	P	W	D	L
FAC	1	1	0	0
F	1	0	0	1
Total	2	1	0	1

Tony Waiters

App	Tony Waiters	Opponent	Date	Fix	Result
1	England	Belgium	21/10/1964	F	D 2-2
2	England	Wales	18/11/1964	BC	W 5-1

As one of three Blackpool players in Alf Ramseys preliminary 40 player squad Tony Waiters was clearly in the managers thoughts ahead of the 1966 World Cup. During the calendar year of 1964 he was called up on 10 occasions and selected 5 times. Two of those appearance came at Wembley in the space of just 4 weeks in October and November.

Selection for the friendly international against Belgium made him the fourth Blackpool keeper, after Alex Roxburgh, Joe Robinson and George Farm, to play at Wembley and the third to do so for his country. When Ramseys preliminary squad of 40 was announced on 7 April 1966 Waiters was 1 of 5 goalkeepers named. On the 6 May 1966 Ramsey announced the names of the 28 players who would report pre-tournament training and Tony Waiters was one of the 12 players cut from the 40 and asked to be on stand-by in the event of an emergency.

Wembley Record				
Status	P	W	D	L
F	1	0	1	0
BC	1	1	0	0
Total	1	0	1	0

2 Appearances

Steve Mciiiharghey	Mike Davies
Paul Groves	Dave Bamber
Phil Horner	Andy Garner
Ian Gore	David Eyres
Tony Rodwell	Trevor Sinclair

App	Opponent	Date	Fix	Result	Penalties
1	Torquay United	31/05/1991	PO	D 2-2	L 4-5
2	Scunthorpe United	23/05/1992	PO	D 1-1	W4-3

Forty eight years after the glory and drama of the 1953 FA Cup Final Blackpool were back at Wembley. While the occasion was not as glorious the drama certainly was. Remarkably, just under twelve months later the Seasiders returned to the famous old stadium and repeated the drama, editing the script to produce a different outcome to the end of the performance.

Whereas the clubs 1953 FA Cup Final performance had been overseen by players of immense talent and reputation the play-off final appearances of 1991 and 1992 featured players who had vastly different experiences and spent most of their careers in the bottom two divisions of the football league. That Blackpool had reached Wembley again after such a period exampled the changes in the game. Introduced in the 1980's as a method of restructuring the four divisions of the Football League their popularity saw refinement to their purpose and provided opportunity for more players and fans to share the Wembley experience.

While the Wembley experiences provided a talented youngster like Trevor Sinclair a platform from which he progressed to appear in the World Cup finals 10 years later, others were experiencing the highpoint of their respective careers. That 10 players from the 1991 final returned for the 1992 performance indicates Blackpool had a settled squad at that time.

The lows and highs of performance on the Wembley stage were exampled by Dave Bamber with the low of his penalty shoot-out miss in 91 final to the high of scoring in 92 final. Paul Groves became only the second Blackpool captain, after Harry Johnston, to lift a trophy a trophy at Wembley.

One club man Mike Davies became the first Pool player to be substituted twice at the venue while rising star Trevor Sinclair became the first to make two substitute appearances. Paul Groves and Andy Garner scored in both shoot-outs while Steve McIlhargey saved a spot kick on both occasions.

	Wembley Record			
	P	W	D	L
POF	2	0	2	0
PSO	2	1	0	1

Keith Southern

App	Keith Southern	Opponent	Date	Fix	Result
1	Blackpool	Yeovil Town	27/05/2007	POF	W 2-0
2	Blackpool	Cardiff City	22/05/2010	POF	W 3-2

One of the most underrated players to wear a tangerine shirt Keith Southern arrived at the seaside on a free transfer from Everton in July 2002 and departed ten years later to join Huddersfield Town. As one of the few players to play for Blackpool in the top three tiers of English football the fact he was as effective in the premier league as in league one was testament to his professionalism.

There were lows along the way with niggling injuries and not making the bench for the 2004 LDV Vans Trophy final. By then Simon Grayson had arrived as a player and in 2006 took on the managers role. Once early season signings had settled Gnashers formed a central midfield partnership with Claus Jorgenson that provided a solid foundation for the managers 4 4 2 formation.

With a career tally of 35 goals spread over 10 season his knack of scoring important goals was possibly under appreciated. In 2004 he quietened a Hillsborough crowd with a goal to put the Pool 3-0 up on aggregate in the LDV Vans semi-final. His winning goal in a 2-1 win at Cheltenham in April 2007 confirmed a play-off place with two games to spare and his goal in the home leg of the semi-final against Oldham brought the new Wembley Arch into sharp focus for the tangerine faithful.

Having played his part in the play-off final win over Yeovil Town he became the first Blackpool player to score in the second tier of English football since Bob Hatton in May 1978. With his goal earning the seasiders a 1 0 win at Leicester City a new chapter in the history of Blackpool Football Club had begun.

His approach and work rate remained undiminished and the 2009-10 season saw him form a highly effective midfield partnership with David Vaughan and Charlie Adam. Having helped the Pool secure a play-off place his equaliser in the semi-final first leg against Nottingham Forest at Bloomfield Road lit the blue touch paper for a sensational play off campaign.

With a man of the match performance in the final and promotion achieved Gnashers, like defensive colossus Ian Evatt were on the verge of wearing the tangerine shirt in 3 different divisions. It was no surprise to the tangerine faithful that he was just as effective in the premier league as he had been in league one.

After the disappointment of relegation, the 2011-12 season saw him competing for a place along with Barry Ferguson, Angel Martinez and Ludovic Sylvestre. His final competitive appearance in a tangerine shirt was as a second leg play-off semi-final substitute against Birmingham City. Although included in the match day squad for another Wembley visit, he was an unused substitute, adding his name to the list of seasiders who had two appearances at the famous stadium.

Wembley Record				
	P	W	D	L
POF	2	2	0	0
MOM	2010 Championship Final			

2 Appearances

Matt Gilks

Alex Baptiste

Stephen Crainey

Stephen Dobbie

App	Opponent	Date	Fix	Result
1	Cardiff City	22/05/2010	POF	W 3-2
2	West Ham United	19/05/2012	POF	L 1-2

Wembley Record				
POF	2	1	0	1

Alongside Ian Evatt and Keith Southern in the 2010 Championship Play-off winning side were a further four players who went on to make a second Wembley appearance in 2012. Matt Gilks, Alex Baptiste and Stephen Crainey were signed by Simon Grayson following the 2007 league 1 play-off success. By contrast Stephen Dobbie was a player who kept finding his way to the seaside in loan spells from his parent club Swansea City.

Matt Gilks was signed to compete for the keepers jersey with Paul Rachubka following the clubs return to the championship. By the time Ian Holloway stepped into the managers chair at Bloomfield Road Gilks was keen to leave the seaside. Dissuaded from doing anything rash he became established as the first choice keeper before moving on in 2014 as back up keeper at Burnley.

With injury limiting him to only appearing in 18 of the Pools 38 premier league fixture it was seen by many, including the manager, as a significant factor in the Pools relegation. In the 18 premier league games he was between the sticks the Pool accumulated 21 of their 39 points. Had he been fit for all 38 games who knows?

His performances in the premier league earned him international recognition with regular call ups for Scotland during his time at Blackpool. In August 2013 he returned to Wembley as an unused substitute for Scotland in a friendly fixture which they lost 3 – 2 Also among the unused substitutes for Scotland that day were Charlie Adam and Barry Bannan who both featured on that glorious day underneath the Wembley arch in May 2010.

Stephen Crainey had tasted International, Champions League and Premier League football before signing for Blackpool in 2007. With more than half of his senior career games played and all 4 of his career goals scored for Blackpool his performances saw him recalled to the Scottish squad and went on to double his tally of international caps from 6 to 12.

A veteran of over 600 senior first team appearances for several clubs since his league debut for Mansfield Town in the 2002/03 season Alex Baptiste was another player who had the best days of his career in a tangerine shirt. Signed by Simon Grayson at the start of the 2008/9 season he went on to make more than 150 first team appearances in a five year period.

Predominantly a central defender he was at the heart of the Blackpool defence alongside Ian Evatt in their play-off finals of 2010 and 2012. His versatility was demonstrated when he made his premier league debut in the right back position and scored in a 4 0 win at Wigan to see Blackpool top the Premier League.

While Gilks, Baptiste, Crainey were cornerstones pf the Blackpool defence for several seasons, Stephen Dobbie had the element of a boomerang about him. Having fallen out of favour at Swansea City he arrived on loan at Bloomfield Road for the first time to compete for the striking positions with the likes of Gary Taylor-Fletcher, D J Campbell and Brett Ormerod. He proved to be a highly effective impact player, invariably contributing as a substitute.

In the second leg of the 2010 play-off semi-final at Nottingham Forest and the aggregate score tied at 3-3 he scored the goal that gave Blackpool a lead they would not relinquish. Another substitute appearance came in the final as the Pool returned to the top tier . Expectation was that his loan spell would lead to a permanent transfer.

A change of manager at Swansea resulted in Dobbie remaining at his parent club. Having helped Swansea to promotion via the play-offs in 2011 Dobbie fell out of favour again and Holloway brought him back to the seaside for a second loan spell.

Just as it had two years earlier a semi-final goal from Dobbie brought Wembley on to the horizon and the Premier League beckoned once again. Sadly, for the first time in their play-off history the seasiders left the Wembley turf after ninety minutes having been beaten. In the 2013-14 season he returned for the third time as the Pool struggled to avoid relegation from the championship.

After five prolific seasons in Scotland with Queen of the South Dobbie returned to the Fylde coast to spend his final season as a professional footballer a short hop down the M55 at Mill Farm, home of AFC Fylde. Having ended his playing career, he returned to Bloomfield Road in July 2022 as a coach to the Blackpool's Development squad.

Wembley Record				
Status	P	W	D	L
POF	2	1	0	1

1 Appearance

Of the one hundred and nine players to have appeared at Wembley Stadium for club or country while playing for Blackpool Football Club thirty-one of them played there on two or more occasions. The remaining seventy-eight are listed here in their date order of appearance.

Frank O'Donnell	Scotland	England	09/04/1938	BC	W 1-0
Dai Astley	Wales	England	18/04/1940	W	W 1-0
Alex Roxburgh	England	Wales	25/09/1943	W	W 8-3

Each of these three players established a first in the rich history of Blackpool Football Club. For Frank O'Donnell he had the distinction of being the first Blackpool player to tread the Wembley turf in a competitive game. Dai Astley featured in the first ever Welsh national team to visit the Twin Towers while Alex Roxburgh became the first to take his place between the posts.

Manchester United	24/04/1948	FAC48	L 2-4
Joe Robinson			
John Crosland			
Alec Munro			
George Dick			
Walter Rickett			

Of the 9 seasiders to venture on to the turf for the first time in the clubs Wembley debut 5 of them were doing so for the one and only time. Joe Robinson had signed for Blackpool in July 1946 and bided his time in the reserves until first choice keeper Jock Wallace left to sign for Derby County in January 1948. Robinson made his first team debut in the FA Cup third round tie against Leeds United and remained between the posts for the rest of the season.

Having conceded just 1 goal in the 5 FA Cup ties against lower and non-league opposition Joe was beaten 4 times as the Pool came up short on their Wembley debut. Having started between the sticks the following season he was to make way for arguably Blackpool's greatest ever goal keeper, George Farm.
Like many players of this era Johnny Crosland was a player who didn't command a regular first team place but rarely let the team down. Signed as a centre half the consistency of Eric Hayward and versatility of Harry Johnston meant first team appearances were rare. Having not made a first team appearance in the 1947-48 season injury to the regular left back, Ron Suart,

ruled him out for the remainder of the season and Johnny Crosland stepped into the breach. Having swelled his career tally of league appearances from 4 to 6 he was selected to make his seventh first team appearance, and FA Cup debut, in front of 99,000 people.

Having signed for Blackpool and made a goalscoring debut in March 1937 Alec Munro was close to a Wembley debut in 1938 when called up for Scotland along with club mates Willie Buchan and Frank O'Donnell. In the event O'Donnell was selected and "pee wee" as he was known had to wait another 10 years for his Wembley debut.

Signed by Blackpool at the start of the 1946-47 season George Dick made his mark with a debut goal against Arsenal. Having worn every shirt in the forward line bar the number 7 he established himself as the number 10 (inside-left) and scored the Pools first goal of their FA Cup campaign in the third round tie against Leeds United. His seventh FA Cup appearance for the seasiders saw him make his Wembley debut and his final appearance for the club.

Born in Sheffield Walter Rickett played for both United and Wednesday with a spell by the seaside in-between. Signed in mid-season his first experience of Blackpool's 1948 FA Cup run came in the quarter-final win at Fulham. Having made his Wembley debut on the left wing the following season saw him used across the forward line before the blue side of Sheffield secured his services.

| Bill Slater | Newcastle United | 28/04/1951 | FAC51 | L 0-2 |

Although probably better known for his achievements as a Wolverhampton Wanderer, Bill Slater signed for Blackpool as a 16 year old amateur in 1944. Making his first team debut in the 1949-50 season he earned a place in the tangerine record books with a goal against Stoke City after just 12 seconds. He became a first team regular in the double chasing 1950-51 season culminating in a Wembley debut in the FA Cup final.

Having moved on to a Wolves side that claimed three league titles and twice finished runner-up in the 1950s he saw the disappointment of 1951 FA Cup final defeat transformed into the elation of victory when captaining the Wanderers to victory in the 1960 FA Cup final.

Cyril Robinson
Ewan Fenton

In his 4 years with Blackpool Cyril Robinson was what nowadays would be called a fringe player. First team appearance were rare due to quality and consistency of players like Hughie Kelly. In the final home game of the Football League season Kelly had the misfortune to suffer a broken ankle. As a result, Cyril made his second league appearance of the season in the final league game. In only his third first team appearance of the season he proved to be a more than adequate replacement on the greatest day in the clubs history.

In Robin Daniels 1971 Official Club History Ewan Fenton was referred to as Mr Reliable. Signed by Blackpool in September 1949 first team opportunities were limited during the early part of his time at the seaside due to formidable half back line of Johnston, Hayward and Kelly. The retirement of Eric Hayward at the end of the 1951-52 season saw Harry Johnston switch from right half to centre half and presented an opportunity that was taken with aplomb by Mr Reliable.

Having established himself as a first team regular and made his Wembley debut in the 1953 final his reliability and consistency of performance helped the club achieve two top five finishes and saw him captain the side for a spell. Having started his footballing journey in Scotland and spent the bulk of it in England, he had spells playing in Wales and Northern Ireland before becoming the second ex-Pool player, after Ernie Taylor, to feature in the European Cup, while playing for Limerick in Ireland

| Glyn James | Wales | England | 18/05/1971 | BC | D 0-0 |
| Tony Green | Scotland | England | 22/05/1971 | BC | L 1-3 |

The disappointment of relegation at the end of the 1970-71 season was tempered for Messrs James and Green as their fine form earned them call ups to their national teams for the British Championship. Selection for Wales saw Glyn James become the third Blackpool player, after Dai Astley and Alan Ball, to be involved in a goalless draw at Wembley while Tony Green was the last seasider to feature in the world's oldest international fixture.

| Derek Spence | N Ireland | England | 07/02/1979 | ECQ | L 0-4 |

On his way to becoming Blackpool's most capped Northern Ireland international Derek Spence became the first seasider to feature in a European Championship qualifying fixture at Wembley. In making his Wembley debut he became the first Pool player to feature as a substitute in a competitive fixture when replacing Billy Caskey of Derby County in the fifty second minute.

Having been capped while at Bury prior to joining the Pool and while at Southend he became the first player to be capped by his country before, during and after his time as a Blackpool player.

Opponent	Date	Fix	Result	Penalties
Torquay United	31/05/1991	D4PO	D 2-2	L4-5
Alan Wright - Mark Taylor				

Alan Wright started his professional career on the Fylde Coast with Blackpool and finished it nine miles down the coast playing non-league football for Fleetwood Town. In between he became Kenny Dalglish's first signing as manager of Blackburn Rovers and made more than 250 premier league appearances for Aston Villa. In 1996 he made a second Wembley appearance as a member of Villa's league cup winning side.

Having joined Blackpool from Hartlepool at the start of the 1986-87 season Mark Taylor was a regular goal scorer in his first two seasons with the club. Injury at Huddersfield in December 1987 saw him miss the remainder of the season and the entire 1988-89 relegation season. His return for the 1990-91 season saw him start the season on the bench before a month on loan at Cardiff City saw him starting games and scoring goals. On returning to Bloomfield Road, he again became a regular starter concluding the season with a Wembley debut.

Opponent	Date	Fix	Result	Penalties
Scunthorpe United	23/05/1992	PO	D 1-1	W 4-3
Dave Burgess, Mitch Cook, Jamie Murphy				

With ten of the twelve Wembley debutants from 1991 returning for a second appearance on the Wembley stage there were three debutants as the seasiders returned to the twin towers for the fifth time in their history. There were two changes to the 1991 starting eleven as Dave Burgess, who had missed the previous season through injury, had reclaimed the right back slot from Mike Davies.

With Alan Wright having vacated the left back slot in the season Dylan Kerr had been loaned from Leeds and created quite an impression with the tangerine faithful. With Leeds not willing to extend his loan to the end of the season the Pool signed Mitch Cook, a member of Darlington's fourth division championship winning side from the previous season to fill the gap. With one hundred and twenty energy sapping minutes player under the twin towers He stepped up to take the Pools first penalty and drilled it home to lay the foundation for a successful shoot-out.

At the end of the 1991-92 regular season the Pools third debutant, Jamie Murphy had made just one first team appearances in an FA cup tie against Hull City. By the 23 May 1992 he had made two further appearances, as a substitute in the play-off semi-finals against Barnet. In the play-off final his appearance as sixty-eighth minute substitute in place of Mike Davies meant his Wembley debut preceded his football league debut.

Yeovil Town - 27/5/2007 - L1PO - W 2-0
Paul Rachubka
Sean Barker - Robbie Williams - Micheal Jackson - Adrian Forbes
Claus Jorgenson - Keigan Parker - Andy Morrell - Wes Hoolahan
David Fox - Simon Gillett - Scott Vernon

Blackpool's first visit to the new Wembley Stadium saw twelve players make their only appearance at the venue while with the club. Ian Evatt and Keith Southern would both make the journey again as would Ben Burgess, a none playing substitute on this occasion. The only survivor in this squad from the 2001 league play-off campaign was Danny Coid who, like Big Ben, was a non-playing substitute on this occasion. With the 2001 final played at the Millennium Stadium in Cardiff, Danny Coid didn't get to tread the Wembley turf in anger.

Michael Jackson became the third Blackpool captain to lift a trophy at Wembley while Paul Rachubka became the first keeper to record a clean sheet at the stadium. The use of the loan market was becoming increasingly important and the two loanees in the final squad, Robbie Williams and Simon Gillett, both made their mark. Williams, a left back, had the distinction of scoring in his final appearance for the club while Gillett, who had a loan spell at Bournemouth in between two separate loan spells at Blackpool scored both for and against the seasiders during the regular season.

Despite making 17 first team appearance the following season the superb goal Keigan Parker scored to end the 29 years wait for promotion proved to be his last in a tangerine shirt.

Cardiff City - 22/05/2010 - CPO - W3-2
Seamus Coleman - Gary Taylor-Fletcher - David Vaughan
D J Campbell - Charlie Adam - Brett Omerod
Barry Bannan - Ben Burgess

Of the 14 played involved in this remarkable day 8 Of them would do so for the only time as a Blackpool player. Seamus Coleman and Barry Bannan returned to their parent clubs at the end of their loan spells. DJ Campbells second successful loan spell led to a permanent transfer and became the first Blackpool player reach double figures in the top divisions goal scoring charts since Micky Burns 40 seasons earlier.

Ben Burgess, an unused substitute in the league 1 play-off final of 2007 made it on the pitch for the last time in a tangerine shirt. Gary Taylor-Fletcher and David Vaughan, both signed by Simon Grayson flourished under the management of Ian Holloway and enjoyed a superb 2010-11 seasons in the premier league. Transfer to Sunderland saw Vaughan remain on the premier league. Unfortunately, injury denied GTF a second Wembley appearance with the Pool in 2012.

Charlie Adams performances earned him a recall to the Scotland squad and a move to Liverpool while Brett Ormerod completed the rare feat of playing and scoring in all four divisions of the football league for the same club.

Richard Kingson	Ghana	England	29/03/2011	F	D 1-1

A return to top flight football saw the number of international appearances made by Blackpool players increase considerably. The first ever meeting between England and Ghana saw Richard Kingson become the first Blackpool player since Derek Spence in 1979 to appear in an international at Wembley and the first to do so under the arch.

Of the nine debutants to take to the Wembley stage 2012 Neal Eardley was one of Ian Holloways first signings as Blackpool manager. Injury to Eardley in the previous championship campaign saw Seamus Coleman arrive on loan and claim the right back slot in the final. Ludovic Silvestre, signed following promotion to the premier league, became a regular following relegation and the departure of Charlie Adam. Like Ludo, Matt Phillips became a regular starter in the 11/12 season scoring a memorable hat trick in an FA Cup tie against Fylde Coast neighbours Fleetwood Town.

Holloways policy of looking for players of youth, talent, experience and a liking for strikers saw Tom Ince and Angel Martinez fulfil the first two categories. Barry Ferguson and Kevin Phillips brought their experience to the stage while Ronan Bednar and Noah Dicko, ninetieth minute substitutes at Wembley were brought in to provide striking options.

A club record 14 players made their Wembley debuts on this visit. Of the debutants 8 were wearing the tangerine shirt for the last time. Having been in the squad relegated from the championship and league in successive seasons Tom Aldred's Wembley debut ended after 31 minutes. Having left the pitch in tears he had the consolation of being the fifth Blackpool captain to lift a trophy at the stadium. Neil Danns, in his second loan spell at the seaside, and Jordan Flores came to the end of their loan periods. Like Tom Aldred, Sam Slocombe, Clark Robertson, Jack Payne and Ian Black were out of contract and moved on.

Brad Potts third minute goal earned him the distinction of being the second Blackpool player, after Robbie Williams 10 years earlier, to score at Wembley on his final competitive appearance for the club. Although not out of contract, the opportunity to step up to the championship arose on the eve of the 2017/18 season and he moved on to Barnsley.

Of the six who remained the following season Bright Osayi-Samuel who made his Wembley debut as replacement for the injured Tom Aldred departed to play championship football with Queens Park Rangers after just 4 games in league one. Kyle Vassell, Kelvin Mellor, Colin Daniel and Will Aimson all moved on at the end of the 2017/18 season, Mark Cullen, who scored 4 and assisted 3 of the Pools 8 goals in their play-off campaign had an injury hit season and became the last of the 14 to leave in November 2018.

Lincoln City - 29/5/2021 - L1PO - W2-1

Chris Maxwell - Ollie Turton - Dan Ballard - James Husband

Luke Garbutt - Demetri Mitchell - Kenny Dougall - Kevi Stewart

Elliot Embleton - Keshi Anderson - Jerry Yates

Gary Madine - Grant Ward - C J Hamilton - Jordan Thornley

Of the club record fifteen Wembley debutants in 2021 twelve of them would feature for the Pool in their return to the championship for the 2020-21 season. For captain Chris Maxwell it was his second play-off success on the Fylde coast, having kept goal for Fleetwood Town in their league 2 win over Bristol Rovers in 2014. Of the three players who made their final appearances Ollie Turton made a permanent move to Huddersfield Town while Dan Ballard and Elliot Embleton returned to their parent clubs, Arsenal and Sunderland, respectively.

Dan Ballard's performances for the seasiders had seen him capped five times by Northern Ireland during the season while Elliot Embleton made a second consecutive league one final winning appearance in 2022 for his parent club, Sunderland.

Part three – Millenium men

Part three acknowledges the thirty-one players who, but for the decision to redevelop the stadium, would have appeared on the Wembley stage on as many as three occasions between 2001 and 2004. The decision to redevelop Wembley saw those players find an alternative stage, the Millennium Stadium in Cardiff, on which to display their talents.

3 Appearances

John Murphy & Richie Wellens

Of the thirty one players who appeared on the Millenium stage two of the players synonymous with the period, John Murphy and Richie Wellens, joined a select band of seasiders in making three cup final appearances for the club.

An underrated centre forward who combined well with a number of strikers during his seven years at the seaside big John Murphy, courtesy of his goals in the Football League Trophy finals of 2002 and 2004 became only the second Blackpool player, after Stan Mortenson, to score in two cup finals.

That Richie Wellens failed to complete ninety minutes in any of his three cup final appearances was testimony to the performances he produced on the biggest stage. Each time the substitution was made with consummate timing to enable the tangerine army to show their appreciation for his performance.

2 Appearances

**Phil Barnes – John Hills – Tommy Jaszcun – Paul Simpson
Danny Coid – Ian Hughes – Martin Bullock**

Of the remaining twenty nine seasiders who appeared on the Millenium stage seven of them did so on two occasions. With just under ten months between the 2001 play-off final and the 2002 LDV Vans trophy final four of the seven double winners featured in both games. Phil Barnes and John Hills started on both occasions while Ian Hughes and Paul Simpson both came off the bench in quite different circumstances.

Ian Hughes was a first half substitute for injured skipper Ian Marshall while Paul Simpson made his final appearances in a tangerine shirt as a late substitute for Richie Wellens. Having missed the 2001 play-off final through injury Tommy Jaszcun went on to claim two LDV Vans Trophy winners medals.

Having played in 2001 Danny Coid unfortunately missed the 2002 final through injury. In 2004 he returned to the Millenium stage and scored the Pools second goal in the win over Southend. Of the nine players to appear in Cardiff on two or more occasions Martin Bullock was the only one not at the club at the time of the 2001 play-offs.

Bully as he was known to tangerine faithful soon became a fan favourite and certainly made his mark in the LDV Vans competition with a golden goal in the 2002 semi-final and a man of the match performance in the 2004 final.

1 Appearance

2001

Gary Parkinson – Brian Reid – Phil Clarkson – Brett Ormerod
Jamie Milligan – Phil Thompson – Mike Milligan

Of the fourteen seasiders to make their Millenium debut in the 2001 play-off final win over Leyton Orient seven repeated the experience while the remaining seven were to grace the stage for the only time in tangerine. Indeed three of them were Fylde Coast born and spent much of their careers in the area.

Hambleton born Phil Clarkson, known to Pool fans as the ghost, due to his knack of appearing from nowhere to score a goal, played non-league football for Fleetwood Town and found his way to Blackpool via Crewe. Two of the substitutes, Jamie Milligan and Phil Thompson made their professional debuts with the seasiders before moving on to Fleetwood Town and Squires Gate, respectively.

Gary Parkinson and Mike Milligan, were both experienced professionals in the twilight of their careers while Brian Reid, signed by Graham Souness for Glasgow Rangers in 1991 became the second of nine seasiders to find the net at the millennium.

When talking about the fortunes of Blackpool Football Club in the twenty-first century the name of the decisive fourth goal scorer the play-off final, Brett Ormerod, is never far away. One of the hardest working players to wear a tangerine shirt he would become the only seasider to appear on both of the grand stages and, inevitably, score at both of them.

2002

John O'Kane – Ian Marshall – Lee Collins – Chris Clarke
Scott Taylor – Richard Walker

As the Pool looked to consolidate in the third tier faces began to change and ten months on from the play-off success the millennium stadium would see another seven seasiders make their only appearance in tangerine on this grand stage.

With players invariably being signed on shorter term contracts player turnover was on the increase the remaining millennium debutants all arrived during the season and departed before the club returned to Cardiff in 2004. Having been an unused substitute for Bolton Wanderers in their 2001 play-off win Ian Marshall returned to the venue as the Pools captain, and, having lifted the LDV Vans Trophy saw fit to announce his retirement from the game.

John O'Kane, with experience gained across the divisions while playing for eight different clubs, made Blackpool his final destination while Chris Clarke moved on having made his final appearance in a tangerine shirt against premier league opposition, Portsmouth, in the FA Cup.

Lee Collins was a member of the promotion winning squad who unfortunately missed out on a 2001 appearance but gained a starting place on the stage when the Pool returned to the Welsh capital.

Richard Walker had been on loan at the seaside during the promotion campaign and returned on a permanent transfer the following season as the Pool looked to fill the void left by the departure of Brett Ormerod. The player he replaced as a substitute in the final, Scott Taylor, was another signed as a potential replacement for Brett and went on to score more than fifty goals for the club in all competitions.

2004

Lee Jones – Simon Grayson – Mike Flynn – Steve Elliott
Mike Sheron - Tony Dinning – Matty Blinkhorn
Leam Richardson – Steve McMahon

As the seasons rolled on and the Pool continued to occupy mid-table positions shorter contracts and a reliance on experienced pros coming to the end of their careers was a common theme.

Had this final been at Wembley, Lee Jones would have been first Pool keeper to record a clean sheet at the stadium. In the event he became the first to keep a clean sheet in both the semi-final and final of a cup competition,

Simon Grayson came to Blackpool looking to train and maintain fitness, earnt himself a contract, and went on to make 150 appearances in a tangerine shirt and become a significant figure in the clubs history. Mike Flynn arrived at Bloomfield Road having made over 700 competitive appearances and added another 50 to that tally while wearing a tangerine shirt. Steve Elliott was a short term signing who arrived in November 2003 and moved on in July 2004.

Tony Dinning was a much travelled midfield player who played 13 games while on loan from Wigan Athletic between January and March 2004 helping the team to register 5 wins during the period. With 2 of those wins coming against Sheffield Wednesday in the 2-legged northern area final and 1 in the final he returned to his parent club with a winners medal to show for his time at the seaside.

The sixth debutant starter was the managers former Manchester City team mate, Mike Sheron who spent just the one season at Bloomfield Road. Replacing him as a seventy fourth minute substitute was local boy Matty Blinkhorn. With ninety minutes on the clock Liam Richardson and Steve McMahon junior became the thirtieth and thirty first Blackpool players to make an appearance on the millennium stage.

Bibliography

Books

Armfield, Jimmy - Right Back to the Beginning
Headline Publishing – First published in 2004

Ball, Alan – It's all about a ball - First published 1978

Calley, Roy – Blackpool the Complete Record
The Derby Books Publishing Company – First Published 2011

Daniels, Robin – Blackpool Football
Robert Hale & Company – First Published 1972

Gillatt, Peter – Blackpool - On This Day
Pitch Publishing (Brighton) Limited – First Published 2009

Isherwood, Glen - Wembley the Complete Record 1923-2000
SportsBooks Limited

Johnston, Harry – The Rocky Road to Wembley
Museum Press Limited – First published 1954

Matthews, Stanley – The Way It Was
Headline Publishing – First Published 2000

Rollin, Jack - Rothmans Football Yearbook 1980-81
Queen Anne Press

Online resources

England Football Online | The True Story of the National Football Team

The English National Football Archive (enfa.co.uk)

Football transfers, rumours, market values and news | Transfermarkt

Welcome to footballsite

Hopefully, this book will have provided an insight into an element of the Seasiders history and stirred some memories. Whether you have enjoyed this book or otherwise a review would be appreciated. If any errors or incorrect information is spotted, please let me know at:

seasider63@btinternet.com

If anyone has any anecdotes, information, or questions relating to the information in this book, please forward them to the above e-mail address.

Printed in Great Britain
by Amazon

45026492R00116